M000158211

United in the Sixties

Roy Cavanagh MBE & Carl Abbott

Copyright © 2019 Roy Cavanagh & Carl Abbott

All rights reserved.

ISBN- 9781692001711

DEDICATION

Carl Abbott and Roy Cavanagh MBE would like to dedicate this journey through the 1960s to DAVID MEEK, the former Manchester Evening News and Football Pink reporter.

David, though, was really the written voice of Manchester United, via those papers, his massive contribution to the club programme the 'United Review' where he also ghosted the views of managers from Sir Matt Busby to Sir Alex Ferguson, and the many excellent books he wrote on the history of this great club. He originally followed Tom Jackson who was one of the eight eminent journalists killed in the Munich air disaster of February 1958. The message to the masses is a very important one and as far as followers of Manchester United are concerned that was David Meek. He sadly passed away in 2018 at the age of 88.

CONTENTS

ACKNOWLEDGEMENTS

The authors gratefully acknowledge the marvelous contributions to this book from Pete Molyneux and Mike Carney. We also pay particular thanks to Sir Matt Busby, Dennis Viollet, Albert Quixall, Paddy Crerand, George Best, Alex Stepney, Wilf McGuinness, Willie Morgan, David Herd, Nobby Stiles, Tony Dunne and Martin Edwards for their contributions to the book through interviews with Roy Cavanagh.

INTRODUCTION

To write a book there, obviously, has to be a strong pull for the subject to do so. When that subject is often referred to as *'If you lived through the 1960s, and remember it, you were not actually there'* it makes you stop and think.

Well, ROY CAVANAGH MBE bucks that trend by not only remembering it but far more than say the last ten years! He explains;

'Being 12 at the start of the 1960s, and just over a couple of years off starting to work, and ending it at 22 married for three months, the decade certainly formed my life. As Manchester United always played a massive part for me, moving from the relatively recent post-Munich days to seeing them win the European Cup towards the end of it, makes the 1960s a really strong decade in the history of the club.

That their players of that time included goalkeepers such as Harry Gregg and Alex Stepney, a full back in Tony Dunne who was of genuine world-class, a half-back line of such difference in the artistic Pat Crerand, steely Bill Foulkes and at left-half the only Manchester lad who has ever won the European and World Cup in Nobby Stiles shows the calibre of footballers involved. Then you look at the likes of forwards who wore the 7-11 shirts in the 1960s decade. Dennis Viollet, still United's record league scorer in a season and a Busby Babe legend, David Herd a great centre-forward, John Connelly a marvellous winger who would be part of England's 1966 World Cup squad, and then three footballers who are enshrined in the history of the game, George Best, Denis Law and Bobby Charlton. George still the finest footballer I have seen, Denis simply the King and Bobby a legend's legend and like Nobby, a European and World Cup winner.

The life and times of the 1960s certainly changed the world immeasurably. Man landed on the Moon, Music and Entertainment exploded with The Beatles changing music and waking up horizons, the James Bond films giving visions of glamour and excitement, while medical advances changed and saved people's lives. The downside saw violent conflicts and assassinations of people who were changing the world for the better.

I lived through the 1960s and remember it well, hope you enjoy a similar journey through the pages of this book.'

Co-author Carl Abbott was born on 2 January 1963 at the beginning of that year's big freeze. Carl explains the attraction of the decade to him;

'Unlike Roy – I can't say that I was there. My first match was the 0-0 draw in the league cup tie at home to Middlesborough on my eighth birthday in 1971. But Aristotle's famous quote is "give me a child until he is seven and I'll show you the man" and before the decade was out and I reached my seventh birthday in 1970 I have no doubt I was already a United fan forever.

One of my earliest memories was my father seemingly banging his head on the ceiling as United scored in the 68 European Cup Final. As I say in Chapter 10, I was always

1

fascinated by the print we had on the wall by William Papas depicting the celebrations in Manchester on the night of that triumph. In the top corner of the drawing on a scroll beneath an angel's trumpet is that famous eleven: Stepney, Brennan, Dunne, Crerand, Foulkes, Stiles, Best, Kidd, Charlton, Sadler, Aston. I remembered those players long before I could remember my times tables. The stories I heard made the players seem like gods to me. In many ways, they still are, and when you think of the sheer joy that they brought to so many surely they deserve to be.

But despite the glory, there were bad times in the sixties too. For me, football has always been about more than the ninety minutes. There is so much that I never knew about, and as always it has been a pleasure to work on a book with Roy. I believe his memory of the decade is second to none, and it is supported by interviews with most of the key players from that decade. I hope that together we have produced a full account of that most glorious of decades not only detailing the facts and figures of matches but also the lived experience of those that were there.

Chapter 1

AN UNSURE FUTURE

1959-60

As the fifties drew to a close, Britain could look back on a decade of growth. The hardship that followed the war had paved the way to a post-war boom. Rationing had ended in 1954, and in 1957 Harold Macmillan was able to make his famous claim that 'Britain had never had it so good'. In the years between 1955 and 1960, wages had risen by 34% at a time when the real cost of consumer items, barely thought of before the war, such as TVs and refrigerators were falling. Car ownership, although still comparatively rare had seen a 250% increase during the decade. Social change was beginning to take root too, particularly amongst the young which saw the beginnings of a recognised teenage culture. For many in the streets of Manchester and Salford life was still tough, despite this there was a real sense of optimism as the cities entered the 1960s. That optimism was accompanied with uncertainty though, as alongside the economic development much of the old social order was disappearing.

Football, too, was changing. It was still an essential element of working-class life. For Salford lad Roy Cavanagh, what lay in store for his beloved Manchester United was more important than almost anything else. The 50s had been a decade of great success that culminated in terrible tragedy. Against all the odds the team and club had continued – reaching the FA Cup Final in 1958 and finishing 9th in the league. Remarkably the team then went on to finish 2nd in the league in 1959, comparative success though masked fundamental problems at the club. Its financial position was weak, and despite the incredible bravery of all involved with the club post-Munich it was impossible to replace that lost generation. As United entered the 60s that harsh fact was beginning to bite, and so despite the natural optimism of fans, there was a high degree of uncertainty surrounding the future of Manchester United.

The start of the 1960s for co-author Roy Cavanagh is inextricably linked with the Salford or Manchester docks. The bond between the two adjacent cities of Salford and Manchester can be contentious. Especially to Salfordians. The proximity and similarity to each other mean that Salford is often perceived to be part of Manchester. For

Salford lads such as Roy Cavanagh there can be no argument though:

'We are Salford, NOT Manchester! There is no better symbol of the complex relationship between the two cities than 'Manchester Docks' The main entrance on to the docks was on Trafford Road, which I can assure everybody is definitely in Salford! The large white arch which drew you inside though, had the words 'Manchester Docks' blazoned across the top of them because, allegedly, Salford Council did not agree to some of the financial terms, leaving Manchester Council to go forward with the development on their own. I lived very close to those Docks, now, of course, the home of a vastly regenerated area of Salford, known as 'The Quays'. The Quays are now the home of the BBC, one of the few Media Cities in the world, the Lowry Theatre, studios, restaurants and many fine properties which have totally transformed the area since the Docks closed in 1982 just short of its 100 years existence since Queen Victoria had opened it in May 1894. There is just no comparison in living conditions now with when I was growing up adjacent to the docks in the 1950s. Looking back, conditions were unacceptable, but because people had seen nothing better, they were accepted. Now the Salford Quays area has all the amenities people could want.'

'By 1958 the Docks were at their peak with freight carried through its waters of nearly 20 tons every year. The docks brought wealth to the city of Manchester, but that wasn't always reflected in the life of the workers there. Times could be desolate for some people as they would have to hang around outside the white arch just hoping a foreman would catch their eye to give them a day's work. Those times also featured a ritual which I vividly remember as the new decade of the 1960s dawned. On New Year's Eve we would be serenaded by the ship's sirens and hooters and by 31 December 1959 there were plenty of ships in docks. I can still recall as I lay in bed the 1960s were welcomed by the sounds of the ships filling the sky around where I lived, just a couple of minutes' walk away.'

Whilst the sirens of the ships moored at the nearby Docks were still on Roy's mind, it was less clear what was occupying the minds of the Manchester United footballers as they travelled to the North East to play Newcastle United at St James' Park on Saturday 2 January 1960, the first fixture of a new decade. United started the decade in 10th place, having played 24 matches and amassed 25 pts with a goal record of 59F and 47A. The rivals around them then included Preston North End, Burnley, Sheffield Wednesday, Blackburn Rovers, Bolton Wanderers and Fulham. Newcastle were a couple of positions below Manchester United, but they would, no doubt, have been fired up by their manager Charlie Mitten.

He had been a Manchester United legend from their famous 4-2 victory in the 1948 FA Cup Final over Blackpool at Wembley Stadium. Two years later he was turned from legend into villain as he decided to cut and run not just from Manchester United, but from England to go over to South America and ply his trade in Columbia for what were enormous amounts of money at the time. That move had caused a great deal of annoyance to Manchester United manager Matt Busby, and while Matt was a very courteous, civil man, he would remember those times as his side travelled to Newcastle. It would be Charlie Mitten though who would have the most memorable match of his managerial career.

A Day's Soccer

Misery, Magic and Hysteria

By JOHN SCOTT

A WIN at Birmingham with one priceless goal—scored by their new addition, Allen, in the second half—put Tottenham three points clear of rivals at the head of the table: a satisfying start to a new decade.

Preston, Tottenham's nearest rivals in the past weeks, have drifted away. Held twice by Leicester over the holidays, they were trounced 4—0 at West Bromwich yesterday. After a steady period of success, Finney and his colleagues have lost control of the steering.

Burnley, who have slipped above them on goal average, did great things in the mud at Upton Park and won 5—2. But many people fancy Burnley more as Cup winners.

It was an afternoon when a clean white ball soon became a lump of misery to brawny athletes slopping it through the mud. The day's sensation took place at St. James's Park, where Newcastle played wonderful football to beat Manchester United 7—3. The shooting power of White, who scored a hat-trick, and the conjuring tricks of Eastham and Allchurch, caused hysteria in United's defence. Like Burnley, Newcastle will be strongly fancied now for a good Cup run.

A 7-3 defeat would be the largest league defeat of Matt Busby's career, although both Tottenham and Hibernian had scored seven in friendly matches. It was also Manchester United's highest defeat since Charlton Athletic had thrashed United 7-1 at the Valley in the 1938-39 season. It was not a way to start a New Year and certainly not a new decade. Of the eleven who appeared for Manchester United at Newcastle in this inglorious display, four players, Bill Foulkes, Dennis Viollet, Bobby Charlton and Albert Scanlon had been in the plane crash at Munich, whilst Albert Quixall was the record transfer fee between British clubs, so there was a wealth of experience in the team.

Teams: Newcastle United; Harvey, Keith, McMichael, Scoular, Stokoe, Bell, Hughes, Eastham, White, Allchurch and Luke. Manchester United; Gaskell, Foulkes, Carolan, Goodwin, Cope, Brennan, Dawson, Quixall, Viollet, Charlton and Scanlon.

An immediate response was delivered the following Saturday when United travelled to second division Derby County for a 3rd round FA Cup tie. Right half Freddie Goodwin would score United's third goal in this match with a left-foot shot, the same left-foot which had required an operation before the match due to an infected toe. As it turned out, this would be Goodwin's last first-team appearance for the club. United had lost the services of Wilf McGuinness from a broken leg in December, this coupled with the very disappointing performance, and scoreline from Newcastle meant Matt Busby had to act.

BUSBY BABES

FREDDIE GOODWIN

Busby's answer was to pay £30,000 for the hard-tackling West Bromwich Albion and England U23 player Maurice Setters. Many people thought Setters would go into the number six shirt currently worn by young Manchester lad Shay Brennan, leaving Freddie Goodwin in the number four shirt. Brennan had been thrust into senior action for his debut in the emotive FA Cup tie against Sheffield Wednesday 13 days after the Munich Air Disaster, playing in an unfamiliar outside-left position. By January 1960, Shay was occupying the iconic number six shirt which Duncan Edwards had worn before his death in the air crash, with many believing that position could never be replaced.

It was Goodwin rather than Brennan that Setters replaced. For Freddie Goodwin, this would signal the end of his Manchester United career just as it seemed he had finally secured the number four jersey. Goodwin made his debut as a Busby Babe in 1954 but was never quite able to establish himself in the first-team as he had both Jeff Whitefoot and then Eddie Colman in front of him. Eddie had made that shirt his own until his tragic death at Munich when Goodwin had for the next two years filled that position for the club. The signing of Maurice Setters though would prove too much for him, and he joined Leeds United in March 1960. Besides football, Goodwin had another string to his bow. Like many others of his generation he was also a fine cricketer, and in summer played for Lancashire. Even there though he would find a true star playing in his position, this time the legendary Lancashire and England fast bowler Brian Statham.

After the victory over Derby, a further victory in the FA Cup followed. Once again United triumphed over second division opposition, this time winning 3-1 at Liverpool who since 1959 had been managed by Matt Busby's friend Bill Shankly. Victory gave Manchester United an attractive home tie against Yorkshire rivals Sheffield Wednesday. The week before the tie, Old Trafford celebrated its Golden Jubilee on the 13th February 1960. Its opening match had been 50 years earlier against Liverpool back in 1910, a match United sadly lost 4-3. On the same date in 1960, Preston North End were the visitors to Old Trafford for a league match which ended 1-1. The goals were scored by the respective centre-forwards, Dennis Viollet for United and the legend that was Tom Finney for Preston. On a personal note, Tom Finney was one of the greatest forwards Roy Cavanagh has ever seen, appearing in all five different forward positions of the time against United while also being one of England's greatest footballers.

Old Trafford

As Newton Heath Lancashire & Yorkshire Railway Company, Manchester United's first ground was located adjacent to the railway yard on North Road. The club were evicted in 1893 after their landlords (Manchester Deans & Canons) objected to spectators paying an entrance fee. The club then moved to Bank Street in Clayton which was gradually developed to a capacity of around 50,000. However, after United won the league in 1908 and the FA Cup in 1909, they grew more ambitious, and a new stadium named 'Old Trafford' was built. The initial aim was for this ground to have a capacity of 100,000 but in the end, the stadium's capacity was 77,000.

Old Trafford is now one of the most famous sporting venues in the world. It is named after the region of Manchester in which it is located – adjacent to Trafford Park, what was at the time one of the largest and most advanced manufacturing centres in the world. The importance of Trafford Park to the war effort made it a prime target for German bombing raids. The stadium was first hit in December 1940 in a strike that cost over a thousand lives around Manchester. The nearby Old Trafford Cricket Ground, home of Lancashire County Cricket Club suffered more severe damage that night, and the football ground was able to reopen after a couple of fixtures were played at Stockport County while repairs were conducted. The bomb damage that then occurred on Tuesday 11 March 1941 was much more severe though, and the ground would remain closed to first-team football until Wednesday 24 August 1949.

For the period when the ground was closed United relied on neighbours and rivals Manchester City's generosity in allowing them to share their ground at Maine Road. Manchester United were charged £5,000 per year, plus a nominal percentage of gate receipts. At the end of the war, United were able to claim £22,278 compensation from the War Damage Commission to rebuild Old Trafford.

The new ground was almost an open bowl, which was gradually developed with the addition of roofs. The roofs were supported by pillars that obstructed many fans' views, and they were eventually replaced with a cantilevered structure, with the first cantilevered stand being built by local firm Seddon's in time for the 1966 World Cup. The Stretford End was the last stand to receive a cantilevered roof, completed in time for the 1993–94 season at which point the ground became all-seater with a capacity of 44,000. Since this time further tiers and extensions have been added to bring the current capacity up to 75,957. Further development would mean extending the Sir Bobby Charlton Stand above the railway line which runs alongside the ground. Although this is frequently suggested, there are as yet no definite plans to commence what would be a major project.

Saturday 20 February 1960 saw the newly celebrated Old Trafford hold its highest post-war attendance of 66,350 for the visit of Sheffield Wednesday in the 5th round of the FA Cup. Sadly, the vast majority would go home disappointed as Sheffield won 1-0 thanks to a penalty scored by their wing-half Tom McAnearney. With United now out of the cup and mid-table in the League, Matt Busby felt he had to reassure Manchester United supporters. His message in a match programme reflected how he saw the team's progress two years on from the air disaster.

"Our narrow defeat in the FA Cup and a league average of only one point a game adds up to a rather disappointing season for United, and while I appreciate the feelings of our fans in this regard, it is only fair to say that there have been achievements which should not be lost sight of. Personally, I have been delighted with the form of the Central League side. With a game in hand over their nearest challengers, the reserve team is high and dry at the top of the table. The FA Youth Cup team continue to progress, and we are doing all we can at this level to build the reservoir of youthful talent. If we succeed in this matter, that of having two players of equal ability in each position, I feel confident that in the future we can be as prominent in senior football as we have been in the past."

By the end of the season, Matt Busby though would have the satisfaction of seeing his reserve side duly lifting their championship and the FA Youth Cup team, while not winning the trophy, at least reached the semi-final yet again, having done so for all seven years of the competition, winning it in five.

The message was clear. In the 60s just as in the 50s, Matt Busby would once again put his faith in United's young reserves. Players such as Johnny Giles, Alex Dawson and Mark Pearson, had continued their progress from youth level, with all of them appearing for the first team. In the youth side, a young Manchester lad called Nobby Stiles was certainly catching the eye. Nobby, a former Manchester and England schoolboy international, was able to appear with success in different positions and his combative style endeared him to club officials and supporters alike.

It would be Preston North End who ended Manchester United's interest in the FA Youth Cup in 1960, winning 3-0 at their Deepdale home and losing 2-1 at Old Trafford. The Manchester United youth team has always attracted huge interest from their supporters and this season crowds regularly exceeded 20,000 to see the latest potential stars coming through. Besides Nobby Stiles, the 1960 cohort included forwards Ian Moir and Phil Chisnall, with Alan Atherton and Jimmy Nicholson making up the half-back line with Stiles. In later life, Alan Atherton would become the father of future England cricket captain Michael Atherton.

Nobby wasn't the only schoolboy international on United's books. The first-team included a Manchester and England schoolboy international, who was set to break the club goalscoring record that still stands to this day. His name? Dennis Viollet. Dennis was now club captain after his recovery from injuries in the Munich Air Disaster, before that having been an integral part of the famous Busby Babes side. On 25 March 1960, his goals in a 5-0 victory at Fulham took his total in league matches that season to 31, a figure he would increase to 32 from 36 fixtures by the end of the season. The previous holder had been Jack Rowley, who in the 1951-52 league championship-winning season had scored 30 league goals. Jack, affectionately known as 'Gunner' had played in four forward positions for England in his career, and of course, scored two goals in United's 4-2 FA Cup Final victory over Blackpool in 1948. It is incredible to think that Dennis Viollet's record of 32 goals in a league season is still standing in 2019. When you consider the wide range of exciting, world-class forwards Manchester United have had at their disposal over those 60 years it is clear that Dennis Viollet deserves to be remembered as one of United's greats.

Pos	Club	Pld	W	D	L	GF	GA	GAvg	Pts
6	Bolton Wanderers	42	20	8	7	59	51	1.16	48
7	Manchester United	42	19	7	16	102	80	1.28	45
8	Newcastle United	42	18	8	16	82	78	1.05	44

Despite Viollet's goal-scoring exploits, Manchester United would finish the 1959-60 season in seventh position in the League with 45 points from the 42 league fixtures, a drop from their incredible runners-up position of the previous season. They did, however, score 102 goals but conceded 80. The last three results emphasised this situation as United beat West Ham United 5-3 at home, lost 5-2 away at Arsenal then finished the season with style and hope by beating a Johnny Carey managed Everton 5-0 at Old Trafford. Burnley, a team Manchester United had beaten 4-1 on their own Turf Moor pitch in the last game of 1959, won the league title. The average home crowd was more than respectable with an average attendance of 47,138, but that was a drop of some six thousand from the previous season's average of 53,258.

In the 1959-60 season, Manchester United would use 17 players who played at least nine matches. They were: Goalkeepers; Harry Gregg and David Gaskell, right-back Bill Foulkes; left-back Joe Carolan; right-halves Freddie Goodwin (transferred to Leeds in March as noted above) and Maurice Setters; centre-half Ronnie Cope; left-half Wilf McGuinness and Shay Brennan; outside-right Warren Bradley; inside-rights Albert Quixall and Johnny Giles; centre-forwards Dennis Viollet and Alex Dawson; inside-left Bobby Charlton and Mark Pearson; outside-left Albert Scanlon.

At the end of the season, this senior party travelled to North America, undertaking Manchester United's third tour of the States since the Second World War. They would play ten matches in America and Canada, winning seven and drawing one, although the feeling from those who had been on the previous tours of 1950 and 1952 was that the playing standards had not improved. There did not seem to be a lot of interest in the schools and colleges, although this was going to change over the forthcoming decade and beyond.

Chapter Two

THE SLOW REBUILD CONTINUES

1960-61

The 1960-61 season would prove to be one of the most turbulent in football history. The turbulence was accompanied by striking changes in society too – particularly for the young. Elvis dominated the charts – with Now or Never the biggest selling single and the first to go straight into the charts at number one. The satirical show *'Beyond the Fringe'* was playing to packed houses in London's West End. In October 1960 Penguin Publishing were found not guilty of obscenity for publishing the unedited version of Lady Chatterley's Lover, often seen as the start of the 'permissive society'. Televisions were becoming commonplace in the home and in November 1960 the first episode of Coronation Street was broadcast. Now almost part of the national identity, Coronation Street, with its depiction of ordinary working-class families was controversial at the time. Perhaps the most direct change experienced by young men though was the ending of compulsory National Service with the last man being called-up on 31 December 1960 with the last National Serviceman leaving the armed forces in May 1963. Footballers, of course, were all subject to this ruling, with most of the 'Busby Babes' serving in Her Majesty's Forces. Indeed, in 1956 as Manchester United were going all out to win the league, Bill Foulkes, Eddie Colman and Duncan Edwards were all required to play for the British Army in a match against the Belgian Army in Brussels instead of playing in a vital match away at Luton Town! A couple of years later, Bobby Charlton, was signed off sick from his army duties after the Munich Air Disaster, this meant Manchester United had to get special permission for him to play for them at a time when their playing numbers were drastically reduced. This was because, once you were in the Forces, they were your employer not whoever you might work for outside service life. A point of interest, Bobby English would be the last Manchester United footballer to be demobbed from the Forces in March 1961. Looking back to those days, it is perhaps surprising that National Service ended when it was given the state of world affairs with fears that the cold-war relationship between Russia and the USA might breakdown and lead to disaster. A reflection of this was seen in the tens of thousands of people marching against nuclear weapons.

As these changes started to unfold, Manchester United retained the goodwill of their supporters after the disaster of only two seasons previous. Matt Busby and the club board though were aware that improvements would soon be expected. Other clubs were not standing still and weren't afraid to spend money. As the 1959-60 season ended, rivals Manchester City signed a certain 20-year-old forward Denis Law for a national record fee of £55,000 from Huddersfield Town. United though, were not in a strong financial position, particularly after being seriously underinsured for the effects of the Air Disaster of February 1958 and were certainly relying on the favour of club directors, especially a certain Manchester meat magnate Louis C. Edwards.

Louis Edwards was a big friend of Matt Busby; socially, they went for holidays, meals and the theatre together with their wives regularly. Just before the Munich Air Disaster, there was a vacancy on Manchester United's board of directors, which intensified with the death at the team's hotel of George Whittaker the night before the legendary Arsenal match on 1 February 1958. The match, the last of the Babes on home soil, saw United win 5-4 in what is often referred to as the 'Greatest Game Ever'. The death of George Whittaker is reflected in the famous pictures from that match, which show the United players wearing black armbands.

It seemed before this tragedy that another wealthy benefactor and racehorse owner, Willie Satinoff would be the next director for the club. Mr Satinoff travelled with the Manchester United official party to Belgrade for the ill-fated quarter-final European Cup tie with Red Star where he was one of the 23 people killed in the tragedy. Often referred to as a 'fan' that died in the disaster, he was much more than that. At the first board meeting after the disaster, the Manchester United board elected Louis C. Edwards as a Manchester United director. It is generally believed that Mr Edwards's money was behind the record transfer of Albert Quixall in September 1958 for £45,000 from Sheffield Wednesday.

After finishing seventh the previous season, Manchester United certainly did not need the terrible start to the 1960-61 campaign, with only two victories in their first 11 matches. Mind you, the victories were impressive performances, beating the heavy spending Everton 4-0 and a West Ham United side, including a young Bobby Moore, 6-1, both matches at Old Trafford. A brighter note was the debuts of three of Old Trafford's next batch of promising youngsters. Nobby Stiles made his debut away at Bolton Wanderers, playing in an unfamiliar right-back position, Jimmy Nicholson debuted at left-half away to Everton and Tony Dunne, a young Irish lad signed from Shelbourne for a small fee, played his first game away at Burnley. All three players would become full internationals, with Stiles and Dunne going on to become legends of the club in future years.

1960-61 was also the first season Manchester United competed in a competition called The Football League Cup, which still exists but after a raft of sponsorship name changes. United's first opponents were Exeter City away in lovely Devon. Mind you; United were glad to get away with a 1-1 draw before winning the replay 4-1 at Old Trafford. Sadly, the next round saw an inglorious exit from the competition as lowly Bradford City beat United 2-1 at Valley Parade.

Another fund-raising visit from Real Madrid brought a much-needed financial boost together with a chance to see the glamorous sight of European opposition along with a morale-boosting display in a 2-3 defeat. Youngsters Stiles and Nicholson both started with Dunne coming on as a substitute against a side that included legends of the game in Di Stefano, Gento and Puskas. While this match did bring in extra finance, the guarantee to Real Madrid had gone up, and the admission prices were, therefore, increased dramatically above normal matchday prices. Groundside went to 4/6 (23p) from the normal 2/6 (13p) while the main stand seats went to 17/6 (87p) or 25/- (£1.25p) from the normal 8/- (40p). Season tickets, only available in the Main Stand were £8-10-0d (£8.50). For comparison, the average weekly earnings for an adult male manual worker at the time was £14.

BUSBY BABES

ALBERT SCANLON

Matt Busby may well have been a very courteous man as mentioned earlier, always extremely smart with a compact figure, his fitness being vital in his recovery from his extensive injuries in the Munich Air Disaster, but you did not achieve what he did in life without having a steeliness when required. This decade will certainly show this with Matt's dealings with star players such as Dennis Viollet, Johnny Giles and Maurice Setters, but left-winger Albert Scanlon was the first player in the 1960s to feel this strength.

Albert, although born in Hulme Manchester, lived a lot of his life in Salford, and was always respected in the area particularly after his retirement from playing football when he worked at both Colgate Palmolive and the Docks. At the time of Munich, Albert had been strongly vying with David Pegg for the number 11 shirt and had seemed to have won the chase as he had replaced Pegg for the two months before the disaster. The already mentioned last match the team played in England, at Arsenal, was one of Albert Scanlon's greatest games for United. Then, after his return from his injuries in the 1958-59 season, Albert had been pivotal in United's attempt to win the league before they finished incredibly as runners up.

What caused the split between Matt Busby and Albert Scanlon is only conjecture, but certainly Matt felt he had enough forwards and wanted more strong defenders, so Albert was transferred to Newcastle United. The money from the transfer went to pay a British record fee for a full-back with the signing of West Ham United and Republic of Ireland left-back and captain, Noel Cantwell. For Albert, the consolation that one of Manchester United's greatest left-wingers, Charlie Mitten then manager of Newcastle United, wanted to sign him, must have been a big fillip.

Noel Cantwell was the finished article. He was a leader that Matt Busby believed was needed at Old Trafford in his slow, heartbreaking re-build of his beloved Manchester United. He hoped that this tall, elegant, handsome, intelligent man would be the next Johnny Carey or Roger Byrne. Noel had an immediate problem though. He had come from a West Ham United that just thrived on modern coaching ideas from the players, with such as Malcolm Allison, Dave Sexton, John Bond and Frank O'Farrell joining Noel in discussing techniques and new styles of play. He arrived at Old Trafford to find a club still sticking with Busby's famous mantra of *'go out and play, enjoy yourselves'*.

Noel made his debut in a 3-1 victory over Bayern Munich in an Old Trafford friendly, but any boost to the club's fortunes from the signing was immediately cancelled out as bad injuries struck United. First Johnny Giles broke his leg at Birmingham City and then Dennis Viollet broke his collar bone at Cardiff City.

The star of the Bayern victory though had been the still young centre-forward Alex Dawson who scored a hat trick, commencing an incredible run of goal scoring by the Aberdeen born number nine. From 21 November to 31 December, Alex scored three hat-tricks, the Bayern one was followed by hat-tricks against Chelsea and Manchester City over Christmas 1960! In all this season, he would score 23 goals in 35 league, cup and friendly matches for Manchester United, oh and would appear in goal for most of a very famous victory over what would eventually be that season's 'double' winning Tottenham Hotspur side!

United had started December 1960 in 15th position, but they had climbed to eighth position as the end of January 1961 approached, with Alex Dawson's tremendous scoring rate helping enormously. In the seven league matches over this period, Alex scored his two hat tricks on Boxing Day against Chelsea and New Year's Eve against Manchester City, and also goals at home against Preston North End and away at Fulham and Chelsea. He then got two in the 3-0, 3rd round FA Cup victory at Old Trafford against Middlesbrough, so had scored eight goals in three matches when the opposing sides had forwards such as Jimmy Greaves, Denis Law and Brian Clough playing for them, and all goalless! After all this, Alex was then involved in an amazing position change in the match against the team of the season Tottenham Hotspur on Saturday 14th January 1961.

The week commencing Saturday the 14th January 1961 though, threatened to be a momentous one for football in England. The Professional Footballers Association (PFA) would be meeting again during that week to affirm a potential players' strike over the Maximum Wage which was in operation in football, but also the retain and transfer system which stopped players from changing clubs when their contracts expired. It was that which could not be finalised, and so, a players' strike was to be called for 21 January 1961.

Before that, on the 14th, Manchester United were due to host Tottenham Hotspur at Old Trafford and were quietly confident of becoming only the second team to defeat them this season. Tottenham were by then dominating the first division, ten points clear, at a time of two points for a win in those days. A full house of 65,000 was expected, but the Manchester weather was to be the winner this day as a typical fog of the time, intensified by mists forming over the nearby Docks, meant it was impossible to see across the Old Trafford pitch leaving the referee no alternative to call the match off. It was immediately rearranged for the following Monday night, so Tottenham went back home on the Saturday before returning for the game.

Roy Cavanagh vividly remembers the night, which was to leave an impact on him he has never forgotten. *'I was 13 and had gone to the match as usual with my mates, standing on the Stretford End. My father had always told me to make sure that the crash barriers were always behind you as opposed to you pressing against them. About ten minutes before the start, I looked behind, and one of my smaller mates was going to have no chance of seeing much. So, I swopped. Big mistake!'*

'United made a great start to the game and were really giving Tottenham a lot of problems. After 15 minutes, an unlikely man scored the first goal, young Nobby Stiles, playing in the number eight shirt as he was quickly showing his versatility and quickly endearing himself to the Old Trafford support.' Roy describes the moment. *'United were attacking the Stretford End when Nobby put the ball past Bill Brown in the Spurs goal and my world, literally, turned upside down! The crowd swayed uncontrollably behind me, trapping me against the barrier. I must have passed out, as next thing I am being passed over heads down towards the front of the Stretford End and the St. John's Ambulance people. They quickly brought me round and as half time approached asked "did I want to go back with my mates." I turned around and saw this mass of swaying people and quickly said no to the marvellous people from St. John's!'*

Alex Dawson's night was also about to be turned upside down, as United's goalkeeper, Harry Gregg suffered a bad shoulder injury. With no substitutes allowed, somebody had to take over the green jersey, with Alex being the chosen one! Tottenham, remember, were ten points clear and a marvellous side, so to also now be playing against ten men they were really

15

in the game. In the second half, both Alex Dawson and Harry Gregg were to have major parts to play.

Harry came back with his shoulder strapped and went to centre-forward. The Guardian report the following morning tells the story.

'Alas for United, Gregg aggravated the injury to his shoulder and was led off the field and Dawson went in goal. Dawson was still wearing the goalkeeper's jersey at the restart, and there was a great cheer when Gregg, his right shoulder beast bandaged, returned to play at centre forward, a position one understands he has coveted for most of his life. It now remained to be seen whether he could make a fairy tale ending by scoring a goal— preferably the winner. Gregg, who appeared to have read about the deep-lying centre-forward plan, wandered about quite happily and put in one shot that was nowhere near the target, but at least it was an effort and no praise can be too high for him. Dawson also enjoyed himself thoroughly and he made some good-looking saves, especially one from Allen that Gregg himself could not have improved upon. Try as they did, Tottenham could make little headway against a defence that really excelled itself, and in the seventy-fourth minute United were rewarded with their second goal and another beauty it was. Stiles, Quixall, and Pearson made all the running, and when Pearson slipped the ball out to Gregg, he let it run past him before back heeling it into the centre as though he had been doing this sort of thing regularly. Tottenham were bewildered by this astute move— but not Pearson. He brought the ball under control, and Brown had no chance of saving.'

Manchester United were flying, but they were going to have a major problem in their forthcoming games with their star goalkeeper injured. United's crisis though was small beer compared to the looming crisis facing professional football, which was facing the threat of strike action by the Professional Footballers' Association (PFA). Wednesday 18 January 1961 was an important day in the lives of footballers as, after a prolonged five-hour meeting, their threatened strike for the coming Saturday was called off. At a meeting with the Ministry of Labour, the two parties, the PFA and the Football League, agreed that the minimum wage would end. It was also agreed that the regulation that effectively tied a player to a club for life would be finished allowing players to a transfer when they came to the end of their contract if they so wished. The PFA was marvellously led by Chairman Jimmy Hill and Secretary Cliff Lloyd for whom footballers of the time, and later years, deserve their thanks.

It is hard now to imagine the lives of footballers before the abolition of the maximum wage and the introduction of freedom of contract. The world of sport at the beginning of the 1960s was very different from that of today where top sportsmen are rich beyond most people's dreams. For example, earlier that year Yorkshire County Cricket Club had appointed Vic Wilson as their first professional club captain. The Wimbledon tennis tournament was still limited to amateurs (ladies and gentlemen) with professional players forbidden until the tournament went 'open' in 1968. For people in well-paid jobs at the time it was uneconomic to give their job up for a comparatively low-paid career as a footballer, instead many preferred to stay in employment and play in amateur football where the additional 'expenses' would surpass the wages of a full-time professional. Such was the strength of the amateur game that the Amateur FA Cup Final was one of the very few football games to be televised live. The abolition of the maximum wage would change all that.

The Maximum Wage and Retain and Transfer

Post-war Britain faced a desperate economic situation. Indeed rationing continued until 1954. Professional footballers faced all the same privations of working people. Between the wars a maximum wage had been imposed which had been gradually reduced from £10 to £8 a week, and £7 a week in the close season. This remained the maximum wage when football recommenced after the war. For comparison, the average wage at the time was £4. In the post war years the maximum wage gradually increased to £14 (1951), £15 (1953), £17 (1957) and £20 (1958). These rises did not keep pace with inflation and the general rise in salaries. In 1945, the maximum wage was twice the average wage. By 1960, the average wage had risen to nearly £15 and so a footballer earning the maximum of £20 a week earned just 33% more than the average wage. The players union argued that their members were worth much more and eventually under threat of strike action the Football League abolished the maximum wage. Johnny Haynes soon became the first £100 a week player. The system persisted informally though, and teams such as Manchester United and Liverpool set their own maximum wage levels.

The maximum wage wasn't the only grievance settled under the threat of strike action. The other bugbear for professional footballers was the 'retain and transfer' system. This rule enabled clubs to hold onto players against their will at the end of their contracts. The PFA won, in principle at least, on that front too and the strike was called off. It wasn't until 1963 though that a case that had started in 1959 when George Eastham refused to sign a new contract at Newcastle was finally resolved. Eastham had asked for a transfer to Arsenal as his contract came to an end. Newcastle refused the request leaving Eastham with no choice but to move to London and start a completely new job selling cork in Guildford. Eventually though Newcastle conceded and allowed him his transfer. Despite this Eastham believed there was a point of principle at stake and continued the fight against retain and transfer in the courts. In 1963 the courts found in his favour and the 'retain' element of the system was greatly reduced. It wouldn't be until 1995, under the 'Bosman Ruling' that players would be entirely free to leave at the end of their contract without a fee.

With just 72 hours left before the strike was to start the football authorities conceded. The late cancellation of the strike meant that Manchester United could go ahead with their league fixture away at Leicester City. The Leicester programme opposite shows how late in the day the dispute had been resolved. There is no date on the cover, the programme needing printing earlier in the week and the decision to call the proposed strike off only taken late on Wednesday. Mind you, United and debutant goalkeeper Ronnie Briggs probably had wished the game had not gone ahead, as, after a run of eight matches without a defeat, Leicester inflicted a convincing 6-0 defeat on United.

Although beaten six times, Briggs was not really at fault with any of the goals as the whole United team turned in a very poor display, and this when their wage values had gone up 72 hours earlier!

A visit to Sheffield Wednesday for a 4th round FA Cup tie looked hard at the best of times, after the Leicester mauling even more so. United, however, returned to form and produced a fine display in a 1-1 draw with Ronnie Briggs having a competent game in goal. The replay though played the following Wednesday at Old Trafford proved to be a disaster for Ronnie Briggs and Manchester United. In front of a capacity crowd, Sheffield Wednesday won 7-2 which was the heaviest defeat Matt Busby had ever suffered as a manager, following on from the loss the previous week at Leicester by 6-0 which was the highest goal difference defeat he had suffered. Their neighbours Manchester City also had a bad day, losing at Luton Town 3-1 in the same round with Denis Law scoring their goal. What made that even more remarkable was that the previous Saturday as United drew 1-1 at Sheffield, City were beating Luton 6-2 when the tie was abandoned in the 69th minute due to the state of the waterlogged pitch. Incredibly Denis Law had scored all six of City's goals, so went into the record books as the only person to score seven goals in an FA Cup tie and finish on the losing side.

Matt Busby had no choice but to pull young 17-year-old Ronnie Briggs out of the firing line, so with both his senior goalkeepers, Harry Gregg and David Gaskell still injured he signed the England Amateur international goalkeeper Mike Pinner from Queens Park Rangers. Pinner was a Flying Officer in the Royal Air Force, and he certainly provided a reassuring effect for the United defence, although still not with better results. With no chance of the league and now out of the FA Cup, the season virtually ended for Manchester United that February evening. By the time Blackpool beat United 2-0 on Good Friday at Bloomfield Road, it had signalled only one victory in 11 competitive matches, meaning pride was urgently required to settle the frustrations of the Old Trafford faithful.

The poor displays and results changed from Easter Saturday when Fulham came to Old Trafford, United winning 3-1, with the return after long injury absences for forwards Dennis Viollet and Johnny Giles along with David Gaskell back in goal, certainly helping matters. In the Fulham side was England's inside-left and captain Johnny Haynes. He had been the subject of much press speculation that the Fulham Chairman, the London comedian Tommy Trinder, had broken the bank and made Haynes England's first £100 per week footballer – a huge sum at the time, some five times the previous £20 a week maximum. In later times, Johnny Giles recalled a statement Matt Busby had made to the players about this.

'When the news broke about how much Johnny Haynes was allegedly getting paid, Matt Busby addressed us all after training one day to inform us that, in his opinion, we were all worth the £100 he was on. This was obviously good news, well it was until Matt came back and said after consultation with the board, we would all be put on £25 a week and a £5 win bonus!'

Matt Busby was a great friend of the Liverpool manager Bill Shankly, and it is generally thought that the pair of them decided that their players would not be paid the 'extortionate wages' of the colourful cockneys. Indeed, it would be 1966 before a Manchester United player reached the £100 a week Haynes was on in 1961.

The topsy-turvy displays of Manchester United continued until the end of this 1960-61 season. Having had a start of only two wins in the first eleven matches, they went unbeaten in eight towards the end of 1960 and beginning of 1961, then went on another run of only one win in eleven before finishing the season in fine form unbeaten in seven, scoring plenty of goals in the process. Twenty-three goals were scored in those seven matches, including a 6-0 victory at Old Trafford over Burnley, who were the reigning champions. This match was played on Wednesday 12 April 1961, the same day as Russian cosmonaut Yuri Gagarin completed an orbit of the earth in a Vostok spaceship, the first time a human had done so. This feat was another sign that technological progress knew no frontiers and made Gagarin a world-renowned figure. He would visit Manchester three months later to a wonderful reception from the public.

Pos	Club	Pld	W	D	L	GF	GA	Pts
6	Leicester City	42	18	9	15	87	70	45
7	Manchester United	42	18	9	15	88	76	45
8	Blackburn Rovers	42	15	13	14	77	76	43

Despite their erratic form, Manchester United again finished in seventh position at the end of the 1960-61 season, with 45 points from 42 games. On the positive side, youngsters Nobby Stiles, Jimmy Nicholson, Tony Dunne and Ian Moir all debuted, while Johnny Giles, Shay Brennan, Alex Dawson and Mark Pearson, who were not that much older, had become regulars. The FA Youth side though, for the first time, had not reached the semi-finals while the reserves, having been champions the previous season dropped alarmingly to 17th position. Another cause for concern, especially given the club's fragile finances, was the reduction of attendances. The average league crowd fell dramatically from the 47,128 of the previous season to 37,806. The fans would turn out en masse for the big games with over 65,000 for the home game against Spurs, but in those days, fans were much more likely to pick and choose their games., with for example just 23,628 for the home match against Nottingham Forest. The champions of the previous season Burnley, despite their proximity, attracted just 25,019.

A couple of players left the club, centre half Ronnie Cope and Joe Carolan, Ronnie leaving at the end of the season to join Luton Town while Joe went early in the New Year to join Brighton & Hove Albion, as they were then known. Ronnie Cope was a very decent centre-half who had come through the Manchester United youth system, captaining the youth team to FA Youth Cup success one season. He was due to have travelled with the ill-fated players to Belgrade for the European Cup quarter-final tie in 1958. He was only replaced on the Sunday due to a possible fitness doubt over Captain Roger Byrne, which meant Geoff Bent replaced Ronnie Cope on the flight, tragically, Geoff Bent was one of the eight players to be killed. Joe Carolan was the player Noel Cantwell replaced in the side when he arrived from West Ham United which signalled the end for fellow Southern Irishman Joe.

Chapter Three

A STEP FORWARD, AND ONE BACK

1961-62

Although Elvis and American artists still dominated the charts, there were the first stirrings of things to come in the music scene. The British response was, for the time being, led by Cliff Richard and the Shadows but change would come in future years as in Liverpool the Beatles were playing their first concerts at The Cavern. Car ownership grew, and the first E-type Jaguar rolled off the production line. In business, Barclays Bank opened Britain's first in-house computer centre. Despite repeated attempts by governments to put a stop to illegal gambling 'bookies runners' (often young teenagers) would take bets off punters in the back streets and pubs and bring the money to the underground bookmakers. William Hill and Joe Coral amongst others had started this way. In 1961 the rules on betting were finally changed, allowing the opening of the first legal Betting Shops in the UK. A change that later saw United fan Fred Done open his first shop in Ordsall in 1967 with the business going on to become BetFred with a turnover in the billions. The most far-reaching social change was the availability of the birth control pill through the NHS in an Act of Parliament led by Enoch Powell.

After the upheavals of the previous season, the 1961-62 season saw a more moderate rate of change in the world of football. The rebuild for Manchester United was always going to take time; it was more a matter of how long. Everybody would have to remain patient. Luckily in those early days of the 1960s, there was no sign of the social media world which envelopes most of us these days demanding instant solutions to long-term problems. Club officials, players and journalists seemed to all speak the same language, sticking by the unwritten rule that *'what goes on within the club stays between us.'*

If they were to improve though United needed to change, the movement in transfers was slow, partly because money was still tight and also despite the recent victories of the PFA players did not move around at the whim of agents. The change in the law on betting also gave rise to an idea to raise capital to ensure United would be more financially competitive. The new Manchester United Development Association, which was a lottery-type scheme was novel at the time providing one of the first opportunities for public participation in such a scheme. Thus, everyday supporters and the people of Manchester and Salford provided a financial lifeline to the club. Matt Busby highlighted the financial issues the game of football, in general, was facing. *'Last season saw another disturbing drop in*

21

attendance figures throughout the game, with over 4 million fewer spectators watching league football in 1960-61 and because of the lifting of the maximum wage restrictions many clubs are facing a tricky financial future.'

The transfer activity of the summer break of 1961 saw Matt Busby attempt another piece of his rebuilding jigsaw with the move for the Arsenal and Scotland centre forward, David Herd. He was not a newcomer to Matt though, as he was the son of one of Matt Busby's Manchester City teammates during his successful playing time there before the war. Alec Herd was a fellow Scot and a great friend of Matt's. They played alongside each other in the 1933 FA Cup Final between Everton and Manchester City, the first final when footballers had been numbered with Everton going 1-11 and City 12-22. For information, Matt Busby wore 19 and Alec Herd 14, but it was Everton who won the final rather easily 3-0. Twelve months later, the pair had better fortune as City beat Portsmouth 2-1.

During his time at City, Matt Busby would regularly see Alec Herd's son, David, who although born in Scotland had a broad Manchester accent! A great friend of David's was his neighbour, Dennis Viollet, so when he arrived at Old Trafford in the summer of 1961 for a fee of £30,000, he was in good company. Goals in his first two home matches, both victories, against Chelsea and Blackburn Rovers quickly endeared Herd to the Old Trafford faithful. Indeed, after a 3-2 victory in United's ninth match at home to local rivals Manchester City, United were in 2nd place in the table, with only one defeat and a game in hand behind early leaders Burnley.

The Manchester United programme has been called the 'United Review' since the early 1930s and was a must for fans, providing them with updated news on the club in the days before social media. The review would include contributions from both of the evening papers in Manchester at the time, the Evening Chronicle and the Evening News, who both produced Saturday evening sports papers, the Pink and the Green respectively. The 'United Review' for the visit of local rivals Manchester City included its usual look at the junior sides, the 'A' and 'B' teams. It was here that a report of an 'A' team fixture against Stockport County featured for the first time a young Irish winger called George Best having his name in a United programme.

As seemed to be the pattern for the inconsistent United in that era, decent spells of form seemed to be followed by lengthy runs of defeats and draws. From the 23 September victory over City to the end of November, United went without a victory in 11 matches. When a 12th followed in the first match of December, a 5-1 defeat at Everton, the club had plummeted to 2nd from the bottom after having been 2nd from the top. Roy Cavanagh recalls the atmosphere of the time.

The early 1960s were a case of following your team week in, week out whatever the result. The world was not a place of jealousy, wanting what you could not have as what

*you saw you assumed everybody else had. This was reflected in life and such as football.
There, players stayed in the main with their local side, the North West, for instance,
having the likes of Tom Finney at Preston North End, Stanley Matthews at Blackpool,
Jimmy McIlroy at Burnley, Ronnie Clayton and Bryan Douglas at Blackburn Rovers
and Nat Lofthouse at Bolton Wanderers, all playing year in year out wherever their team
where. I was 14 at the time and starting to go regularly to watch United home and away.
The visit to Goodison Park in early December was the usual format for me, a Fieldsends
coach from Salford pay at the gate and watch the game. Mind you in this particular
match as United were 5-0 down at half time Goodison Park was not a happy place to
be, and to compound it all it absolutely threw it down! David Herd did get a goal back,
and it finished 5-1, but United were in the relegation position that night, the first time I
had known them to be in such a dire position.'*

The poor run of results reinforced the need for change and saw two of
Manchester United's younger players who seemed to have been on the cusp
of making the grade at Old Trafford in recent times, leave the club. Outside
right Kenny Morgans, a mere 18 at the time of the Munich Air Disaster
when he had just replaced the excellent Johnny Berry at number seven for
United, never got over his trauma of the crash. He had attempted to
resurrect his form but never got a regular run in the first team and went
back home to South Wales to sign for Swansea Town, as they were then
known. The other young player transferred was perhaps more surprising,
Alex Dawson had seemed to make a real fist of playing at centre forward
for Manchester United, as his goal scoring exploits around Christmas 1960
had proved. Alex was a fine goal scorer with a record of 45 goals scored in
81 appearances for United. Matt Busby though wanted that extra touch of
class in the pivotal number nine shirt, recalling how Tommy Taylor had
made the shirt his own with such distinction, and his move at the start of
the season for David Herd seemed to point the exit door for Alex Dawson.
He moved onto Preston North End, and it has to be said had an excellent
career with them with a fine record of 114 goals in 197 games.

They say a week is a long time in politics, well it was certainly a long
time in football in December 1961 for Manchester United. A 3-0 Old
Trafford victory over Fulham with Herd getting two more goals set the
scene for another visit from Real Madrid. Counting the two European Cup
ties in 1957 this was the sixth occasion the two clubs had played each other,
and it proved to be the first Manchester United victory! David Herd
continued his scoring run with another two goals with young Phil Chisnall,
only 11 days after making his debut in the debacle at Everton getting
United's third, with the Madrid number nine, Alfredo Di Stefano scoring
their goal.

For the third time this season, Manchester United went into a long spell
of consistent results, thankfully, this time a run of 17 matches with only two
defeats, which included seeing the side reach the semi-final of the FA Cup.

As 1962 arrived though, Manchester United seemed light years away from where they were when 1958 had arrived. Since then a confident, successful side with excellent understudies in all positions had been wiped out, the clubs finances were not great, the maximum wage had been lifted, and people were starting to shift in terms of their expectations in life, and in the football teams, they supported.

For the rest of the 1961/62 season, the FA Cup would dominate Manchester United's focus with a refreshing chase of a then still revered trophy. In late January 1962, though there came a very surprising transfer out of Old Trafford, that of the legendary inside left Dennis Viollet. He had been a vital part of the pre Munich side, was (and still is!) the club's leading goal scorer in league matches in a season with 32 and had just belatedly made a rare appearance for England, scoring in one of their last matches of 1961 against Luxembourg in a World Cup qualifier played at Arsenal's Highbury Stadium.

Certainly, the Manchester United performances in October and November 1961 had been far from satisfactory, and while the real reasons for Dennis Viollet's transfer have never been revealed, it does seem that Matt Busby felt he had to make a stand to steady the wobbly ship, and Dennis was the big change he made. Whether it was Matt felt Dennis had too big an influence on the team or not, the fact that when he left for Stoke City, there is no mention whatsoever in the club programme for the rest of that season and the effect it had on Dennis himself was hard to take. Roy Cavanagh, along with the famous boxing trainer Brian Hughes MBE wrote a best-selling book called VIOLLET which fully covered Dennis's glittering career, which still flourished in his time at Stoke City and his later life in America. Here is what Dennis thought of the time he was told his Manchester United career was over.

VIOLLET MOVES –£25,000 DEAL

'One night in January 1962, I was sat at home watching television when the telephone rang. 'Hello,' I answered, it was Tony Waddington the Stoke City manager. He told me he had been given permission to approach me about a move to Stoke. Can you imagine how I felt? I never spoke for a few seconds before Tony sensed my anguish and suggested he call straight around to my house, which I agreed. Obviously, he told me their terms, which were quite good, and I just shrugged my shoulders and accepted my fate. 'Right,' I said,' this sounds great show me the forms, I'll sign for Stoke City.'

'After Mr Waddington left my house, I felt a sudden emptiness come over me, my mind was in a daze, and I just had to speak to Matt Busby. I rang him, and he said yes, he had given Mr Waddington permission to speak to me and said he was sorry he had not informed me first but had been rather busy. Further conversation was not needed; I hung up quickly, although politely. I have said many times how great a manager and

person Matt Busby was, possibly the best manager football has seen. But I will never forgive him for the heartless way in which he had handled my leaving Old Trafford. It felt like an old pair of boots being flung into the corner.'

A remarkable sign of how United were holding the line after the abolition of the maximum wage was provided by the fact that Dennis Viollet doubled his wages to £70 a week while dropping down a division to sign for Stoke City. His departure from Old Trafford shows the hard streak in Matt Busby which did not come to the fore often. Despite his public image, it is not possible to always be the happy go lucky grandfather figure. To run one of the biggest football clubs in the world takes steel. With Dennis Viollet's departure Matt Busby laid down a marker - he was the boss of Manchester United.

The magnitude of the decision can be seen by reflecting on the Manchester United career of Munich survivor Dennis Viollet. A look at his goalscoring record is revealing.

		League	FA Cup	League Cup	Europe	Other	Total	Goals/Game
1	Wayne Rooney	183 (393)	22 (40)	5 (20)	39 (98)	4 (8)	253 (559)	0.45
2	Bobby Charlton	199 (606)	19 (78)	7 (24)	22 (45)	2 (5)	249 (758)	0.33
3	Denis Law	171 (309)	34 (46)	3 (11)	28 (33)	1 (5)	237 (404)	0.59
4	Jack Rowley	182 (380)	26 (42)	0 (0)	0 (0)	3 (2)	211 (424)	0.50
5	Dennis Viollet	159 (259)	5 (18)	1 (2)	13 (12)	1 (2)	179 (293)	0.61
6	George Best	137 (361)	21 (46)	9 (25)	11 (34)	1 (4)	179 (470)	0.38
7	Joe Spence	158 (481)	10 (29)	0 (0)	0 (0)	0 (0)	168 (510)	0.33
8	Ryan Giggs	114 (672)	12 (74)	12 (41)	29 (157)	1 (19)	168 (963)	0.17
9	Mark Hughes	120 (345)	17 (46)	16 (38)	9 (33)	1 (5)	163 (467)	0.35
10	Paul Scholes	107 (499)	13 (49)	9 (21)	26 (134)	0 (15)	155 (718)	0.22

Dennis Viollet still holds the record for the most goals scored in a league season for Manchester United with 32 goals in just 36 games in the 1959-60 season. With a total of 179 goals in all competitions, he is tied with no less than George Best as the club's fifth-highest scorer. Viollet's goals though were scored in just 293 appearances, and with a goals-per-game ratio of 0.61, he has the best record of any of the club's top ten scorers. Albeit that he played during a time when attack was king and more goals were scored, the only other striker that comes close in this list is his eventual replacement and the original 'king' of Old Trafford – Denis Law. The following chapters will tell the story of the impact that Denis made at the club, but before we move to those days, it is only right to give Dennis Viollet the recognition he deserves. There can be no doubt that Dennis Viollet deserves to be considered one of the club's greatest ever goal scorers. Given the players he is competing with that is some praise indeed.

Either side of Dennis Viollet leaving Manchester United, the side had played FA Cup ties, firstly a rerun of the 1958 final against Bolton Wanderers, this time at Old Trafford. Incredibly, despite being close neighbours and long-standing rivals, this 3rd round tie was the only time, other than the final of 1958 that the two clubs had been paired together in the FA Cup. The Bolton legend, Nat Lofthouse, scorer of the two winning goals at Wembley, had now retired from playing but was sat on their bench as the reserve team manager at the time. It looked as though the Wanderers would have another cup victory to celebrate after leading for a long time with a goal by Dennis Stevens. A cousin of Manchester United legend, Duncan Edwards, Stevens was also a Dudley boy and a very fine inside-right who went onto to win the Championship with Everton a couple of years later. It was not until the last seven minutes before United got on equal terms with yet another David Herd goal, before, with virtually the last kick of the match, Jimmy Nicholson scored United's winner.

Besides Dennis Viollet, another Manchester United and England international would be leaving soon, Warren Bradley. Warren played his last game for United in the cup tie against Bolton Wanderers as a late replacement for the unwell Bobby Charlton. Warren had been one of the three footballers amateur football club Bishop Auckland had given to Manchester United in their hour of need immediately after the Munich Air Disaster. Along with famous England amateur internationals, Bob Hardisty and Derek Lewin, the three had helped stabilise United, who remember had eight players killed, two who would never play football again and five still in a Munich hospital straight after the crash. As you need 22 players to field first and reserve team fixtures on the same day, it can be seen that the loss of 15 players stretched the club's resources to the limit.

Warren stayed on after things began to stabilise and, incredibly, went onto play for England at full international level 15 months after his Manchester United debut. He was a clever outside-right, capable of scoring his fair share of goals but a series of injuries and young players pushing through such as Ian Moir and Phil Chisnall meant chances were running out for Warren. He would move onto Bury, although in later years he played a big part for the Manchester United Old Players Association.

The reward for beating Bolton Wanderers was another home tie for United, this time against Arsenal, although as Roy Cavanagh recalls not on the scheduled day. *'Being a big tie, although not all-ticket, a crowd of over 50,000 were at Old Trafford, myself included. After my involvement in crowd chaos against Tottenham Hotspur the previous season, I decided to get a seat ticket for this match in the main stand. Those days the teams came out on the halfway line and I had a great view, until about 20 minutes before the kick-off, from literally everything being in view a mist, becoming rapidly a severe fog, not helped by the smoke bellowing from the special trains which used to bring fans to Old Trafford to the station alongside the stadium. By the expected 3 pm kick-off you could not see the pitch from where I sat, so no chance of the match taking place. The club acted very quickly and gave pass outs to spectators to reclaim for the rearranged fixture on the following Wednesday.'*

When the game did take place, a rare goal from the now captain of

Manchester United, Maurice Setters, settled the tie and put United into the 5th round where the opponents would once again be Sheffield Wednesday for the third successive season and the fourth time in five seasons. In the end, it would take a replay to settle the tie, with both matches attracting capacity crowds of over 65,000. This time, it would be Manchester United's turn to taste success as goals from David Herd and Bobby Charlton provided a marvellous 2-0 victory, and as the draw had already taken place, a 6th round tie away at Preston North End.

Preston had been relegated at the end of the previous season, but since then had bought Alex Dawson from United and promoted a very promising young winger called Peter Thompson, who would develop into an England International and a star player for Liverpool and Bolton Wanderers. They were certainly up for the fight at Deepdale with a capacity crowd, actually far more than the official capacity, which caused severe crowd congestion, seeing an injury-hit Manchester United hold out for a 0-0 draw. The result ensured another massive Old Trafford crowd for the replay, who witnessed two spectacular goals from David Herd and Bobby Charlton to give United a semi-final place on the back of a 2-1 victory.

Tottenham Hotspur were the glamour side of the time, double winners the previous season they had reached the semi-finals of the European Cup where they were due to play Portugal's Benfica, were still in with a chance of retaining their league title and had Manchester United in their way as FA Cup opponents. They also had smashed the transfer record by bringing Jimmy Greaves back from playing for AC Milan in Italy to Tottenham for a fee of just short of £100,000. The tie was to take place at Hillsborough, home of Sheffield Wednesday on the last day of March 1962 with a capacity crowd enduring a near-blizzard in the second half as the heavy rain turned to snow. An early goal by Greaves settled Tottenham, and a shaken United went 2-0 behind after 23 minutes when Cliff Jones scored off a pinpoint cross by that brilliant inside right John White. United though rallied and to their credit, a goal by David Herd with less than ten minutes to go seemed to open a door, only for Terry Medwin to slam it shut with Tottenham's third. Despite their valiant cup run, the report of the match in the following Monday's Manchester Guardian would leave no United fans in any doubt of the work that needed to be done if the club were to compete for major honours.

'Tottenham Hotspur, almost by divine right, again are in the final of the FA Challenge Cup. Apprehension inside Lancashire and expectation outside it were justified to the full at Hillsborough, where Manchester United's only consolation was the charitable margin, 3-1. Not for many years surely has any reputable team in a semi-final been treated with such contempt as was Manchester United's this day. Before the match, one suggested that if United could keep Tottenham on suspicious defence from the start, they might win; in the event Tottenham survived United's opening raid, scored in the

fourth and twenty-third minutes, and for all practical purposes the match was over. In the second-half, Tottenham eased off, and United's "recovery" thus was revealed in a misleading perspective. Tottenham even condescended to allow their opponents to score, but almost at once they restored the margin to discount any impression of a close struggle. Contempt? Nay, this was downright arrogance.'

Once again, the crowds at Old Trafford varied dramatically this season, with the league average falling once more to 33,491. The lowest crowd was against Aston Villa, where just 20,807 loyal supporters witnessed a 2-0 victory. When Ipswich Town, the Cinderella side of the First Division this season, and on their way to the league title, visited Old Trafford the week after the cup semi-final, only 24,976 were present. Those that stayed away missed a fantastic display by United who won 5-0 with Albert Quixall scoring a hat trick. The last home match of the season against Sheffield United on Easter Monday only attracted a crowd of 31,322 who left disappointed as United ended their home season with a 1-0 defeat. Fans could pick and choose their matches in those days. There were very few season tickets located in the main stand. The overwhelming majority of spectators simply paid on the gate. For fixtures against local rivals or attractive opposition, the crowds would remain high with attendances of 57,135 against Spurs and 56,345 against Manchester City. In those days the FA Cup was always a big draw, and these ties produced excellent crowds with 220,000 watching the four home games. By the end of the season though, with Manchester United dropping to 15th, the lowest position at that point in Matt Busby's managerial career, the gates were alarmingly low.

Pos	Club	Pld	W	D	L	GF	GA	Pts
14	Leicester City	42	17	6	19	72	71	40
15	Manchester United	42	15	9	18	72	75	39
16	Blackburn Rovers	42	14	11	17	50	58	39

Interestingly though, the reserves playing in the Central League, had an average playing season finishing 11 of the 22 sides, but still attracted over 100,000 for their 21 home fixtures at Old Trafford, where of course, senior fixtures for Manchester United, i.e. the reserves and the FA Youth Cup should still be played, not farmed out to all and sundry grounds around Greater Manchester! The falling crowds and the decline in form rang alarm bells. Something had to be done if the club were going to re-establish themselves at the top. United's preferred way was through youth, but progress was slow. The team that finished the season was still mainly home produced, only Maurice Setters and David Herd were bought for large fees, full back Tony Dunne only costing £5,000 and still young when he arrived from Ireland. Gaskell, Brennan, Stiles, Foulkes, Giles, Pearson, McMillan and Charlton all Manchester United products, but something was missing. A real glittering of gold was desperately needed at Old Trafford to lift everyone, players and supporters. It was to arrive in the summer of 1962…

Chapter Four

THE ARRIVAL OF THE KING

1962-63

The 60s were, no doubt a period of change in UK and world history. Socially the freedoms and lifestyle of the young by the end of the decade bore little comparison to the early years of the decade. Huge progress was made in the development of technology and the reduction of poverty. The decade was not without its tensions, though. For anyone growing up in the 60s the threat of a deterioration in the Cold War between the USA and Russia into all-out nuclear war was everpresent. Although it was still only 17 years since the end of the Second World War, and while the Korean and Suez Crisis had caused consternation things began to deteriorate further. From May 1960 when Gary Powers flying a Central Intelligence Agency (CIA) on a reconnaissance mission in Soviet Union airspace was shot down, a mission Russia decreed a spy plane, the world changed. Americans particularly, felt threatened, which brought the election of John F. Kennedy as President from January 1961. By August 1961 the Soviet Union had sealed off the Berlin wall, separating East and West Berlin, leaving the world in a very Cold War. Against this background the Campaign for Nuclear Disarmament (CND) had been formed in 1958, and the early 60s saw a series of huge marches in the UK against the development and use of nuclear weapons. October 1962 would see that threat becoming very real in the form of the Cuban Missile Crisis. In response to the failed CIA sponsored Bay of Pigs invasion of Cuba in 1961, the Soviet Union had secretly placed nuclear weapons in Cuba, just 90 miles from the American coast. When photographs of the weapons came to light the US mounted a blockade of Cuba to prevent any further build-up. A diplomatic crisis ensued, and for the only time in history, the American military was put on DEFCON 2 defence readiness (prepared to launch nuclear missiles in under 6 hours). At almost the last minute the crisis was resolved with the Soviets agreeing to remove the missiles in exchange for guarantees over Cuban sovereignty.

Socially, going to the pictures was still a leading recreation in 1962, Manchester then having well over 100 cinemas, from the many in the city centre to outlying districts all of them having at least two. Popular British films that year ranged from Lawrence of Arabia and Dr No. to Carry on Cruising. Films such as A kind of Loving and The Loneliness of the Long Distance Runner were films of the 'British New Wave' portraying everyday life with grim realism. The suicide of famous American actress, Marilyn Monroe on 5th August 1962, caused ripples across the world, Monroe who only recently had made world headlines by singing in a very provocative manner at President Kennedy's birthday celebrations in New York. On the same day, 12,500 miles away in South Africa, Nelson Mandela was arrested by the South African government as their apartheid actions hit home hard. He would be tried and found guilty serving over 20 years in Robben Island Prison.

In the footballing world, 1962 had seen the seventh World Cup held in Chile, with England the only Home Nation that qualified. Northern Ireland lost out in their group to West Germany while Scotland, who on paper had one of their finest sides, lost out in a play-off to Czechoslovakia, Wales likewise in their group against Spain. Manchester United had a heavy involvement throughout the qualifying matches, assistant manager Jimmy Murphy tried to repeat his heroics with Wales from 1958, goalkeeper Harry Gregg played for Northern Ireland, although injury stopped some of his appearances, while young wing half Jimmy Nicholson had games in the competition. Scotland had stars from Tottenham Hotspur, Liverpool, Glasgow Celtic and Rangers, Everton and Manchester United via David Herd, although two of Scotland's star players would become Manchester United players in the 1962-63 season, Denis Law and Pat Crerand. England, who did qualify for the finals, had both Bobby Charlton and Dennis Viollet playing in the qualifiers, although only Bobby Charlton travelled to South America for the finals, scoring against Argentina and playing in their exit, a 3-1 defeat to eventual winners Brazil.

Sadly, Bobby suffered a bad hernia injury while over at the World Cup, which put a dampener on the news which had rocked football during the summer of 1962 in England, Matt Busby's pursuit of the explosive Scottish inside left, Denis Law from Italian side Torino. The decline in United's fortunes so far in the 60s now demanded action. The traditional approach had been to rely on the development of young players. While that had had success through the likes of Nobby Stiles and Johnny Giles it hadn't been enough to stem the decline. A bold statement of intent was needed, and there was none bigger than the signing of Denis Law, for a record-breaking £115,000 fee. The pursuit of the signature of Denis was a protracted affair that played out over the summer period. On 2 May 1962, the Daily Mirror reported that Matt Busby was to meet the chairman of Torino, Angelo Fillipone, in Amsterdam to discuss the terms of a £115,000 transfer. The bid was made and a report a few days later indicated that the deal would be finalised in Lausanne on 12 May. Things did not go to plan though, and there were reports that Torino had sold Denis to their city rivals Juventus and tensions built up between the two clubs until on 22 May negotiations broke down completely. Matt Busby, club chairman Harold Hardman and Louis Edwards stormed out of a meeting in Turin, and an unusually forthright Busby explained: *We have taken this step because we are absolutely fed up with all the intrigue and deceit'.* When asked *'If this explosive ending to the talks put paid to the club's bid for Law?'* Busby replied: *'It is all over as far as we are concerned. We will be leaving Turin for Amsterdam to tie up with the rest of our own tour party. It has been six weeks of hell — and had it gone on much longer I'm sure I'd have had a nervous break-down. We are all disgusted—and that's all I want to say about it at the moment.'*

As it turned out, six weeks of hell was an underestimate. United would get their man, but not for another two months. The man behind the eventual deal was one Gigi Peronace – perhaps the first football agent to operate in England. An English-speaking Italian, Peronace had negotiated the transfers of Jimmy Greaves, Joe Baker, John Charles and Denis Law himself to Italy. Busby and Peronace became friends, and with his help, the transfer eventually went through on 12 July.

Denis had, of course, played previously for Huddersfield Town and Manchester City before joining the movement of players from Britain to Italy. By the start of the 1962 season, Law, Baker, Hitchens and Charles had all returned. John Charles was a magnificent footballer, genuine top class, able to play as a centre forward or centre half with ease. His return to Leeds United, then struggling in Division Two, meant they had to hike their admission prices, their season tickets, for example, going to £10-10-0d (£10-50p), over two pounds dearer than Manchester United supporters would be paying to watch Denis Law in the First Division.

It is difficult to overestimate the importance of the signing of Denis Law for Manchester United. Although things would still get worse in the League, the signature marked the beginning of United's revival and the start of their march to the glory that would culminate in that glorious night at Wembley in May 1968. Denis Law's league debut for Manchester United was on 18th August 1962 against West Bromwich Albion at Old Trafford. He scored within ten minutes adding to an earlier goal from David Herd as United made a flying start to the season. Sadly, West Bromwich Albion pulled the goals back to earn a 2-2 draw, but the crowd of over 50,000 had seen enough to notice the gem that had arrived at Old Trafford. Roy Cavanagh was one of that crowd and recalls the legend that became Denis Law;

'It is not an idle statement to say that in the 65 years of watching Manchester United, there has not been a better signing than Denis Law. The Busby Babes before, Bryan Robson and Eric Cantona later had very similar effects, but Denis was the massive flame that lit Manchester United after four years of dark, tired times. As a 15-year-old I immediately felt a light appear, not just at Old Trafford but in life. Denis just looked a million dollars, his red shirt fit tighter, his shorts had fashion about them and wearing white socks, to go with his blond hair seriously gave him a god-like appearance! That was all off the pitch; on it, he exploded every time you saw him. Quick, brave, deadly in the penalty area, United had a leader, like a man leading a rally way out in front of everyone else, he totally inspired. Many get called Kings; Denis Law is King of Old Trafford.'

It wasn't just Roy Cavanagh that was excited by the appearance of Denis Law in a red shirt. The attraction of Manchester United to football followers had been strong since the return of the game in 1946 after the Second World War, recent years though had seen that decline but a signing like Denis Law enabled United to recapture their glamour. At the time almost all matches were 'pay at the gate' and away matches were quickly sold out of reserved seating and then ground capacities reached before the gates were shut. The first two away matches for United with Denis Law playing for them, drew crowds of 69,000 at Everton and 62,000 at Highbury - both matches finishing 3-1, a win to United at Arsenal and a defeat at Everton. Everton had spent a lot of money on their squad and came to Old Trafford the week after and won again, this time by the only goal, a second-half penalty from Roy Vernon. They would go on to win the league title this season.

Despite the signing, Manchester United's form was certainly not what had been anticipated. Denis Law himself quickly got into goal-scoring action, but further away defeats followed at Bolton Wanderers and newly promoted Leyton Orient, managed by former United and Ireland great, Johnny Carey. A Manchester United legend whose biography 'Gentleman John' was completed by co-authors Carl Abbott and Roy Cavanagh in 2018. Events over a couple of weeks in mid-September summed up the roller coaster times for both the club and the supporters. They covered home matches with Manchester City and Burnley in the league and two prestigious friendlies away at former European Cup winners Real Madrid and at home to the present European Cup holders Benfica.

Manchester City had suffered a poor run of results at Old Trafford in recent years. They came to Old Trafford bottom of the table with the recently opened betting shops of Manchester offering odds of 4/1 about their chances of victory. City fans that took that bet left the stadium happy as they recorded a 3-2 win. City went 2-0 up at half time thanks to goals from Joe Hayes and a Peter Dobing penalty. With rain pouring down, Denis Law got into the act with two great goals at an admiring Stretford

End which seemed to have earned United a deserved point. But, right at the last kick City's new centre forward Alex Harley burst through to hold off Bill Foulkes and plant the ball into United's net for the winner. There would be further Derby Day drama late in the season in the return match.

During the following week, Manchester United visited Madrid to play a testimonial for Jose Zarraga. In poor form at home and having never beaten their Spanish foes, they staggered the football world by winning 2-0 in Madrid. One man, however, Denis Law was born to play on this football stage and although he did not score the thought of 80,000 Madrilenos baying at him lifted his performance. With a still young Nobby Stiles padlocking an ageing Alfredo Di Stefano United turned their delightful football into goals from Mark Pearson and David Herd.

You would have thought that the buzz of defeating the former five-time champions of Europe on their own pitch would have lifted spirits as Manchester United returned to Old Trafford to play Burnley. However, a fine Burnley side tore United apart and won easily 5-2 with a John Connelly hat-trick showing the type of form and skill which would make him a Manchester United player later in this decade.

What mood though would this leave Manchester United who three days later were due to play the current European Champions, Benfica from Portugal? The friendly match had been arranged to celebrate the official opening of the bench seats at the back of the now covered Stretford End. Roy Cavanagh recalls that night and times in the Stretford End.

'A covered Stretford End reminded me of how it used to be, a giant open, sprawling mass of people. I still well remember my Uncle Tom taking me to watch the title decider of the Busby Babes in 1956 against Blackpool, Stan Matthews and all. We just got in before the gates were closed with thousands locked out and finished up stuck right at the back. With me being nine years old totally unable to see anything in front, turning around to see a local works team Glovers Cables playing on their pitch which was in those days right behind the Stretford End where the car parks are now. I then still had the bad memories of getting crushed against Tottenham a couple of years earlier, so it was with more comfort that I took my place in those seats alongside my father Albert, it would be the last time we went to a United game together.'

Benfica were a fantastic side and their star 20-year-old inside-right Eusebio did not disappoint the crowd as he scored twice in a great match, but United had their own star inside-forward in Denis Law, and he got one of United's goals in the 2-2 draw. United wore all white on the night, allowing Benfica to play in their red colours, surely this result would be the one to turn United's season around after matching two of Europe's finest sides in a week?

A 1-0 defeat on Saturday at Sheffield Wednesday not only ruined that thought but pushed Manchester United closer to the bottom of the First Division, the only consolation being City were actually bottom! The return of Bobby Charlton from injury the week after, playing alongside Denis Law for the first time, also did not have an immediate effect but in late October 1962 football had to take a large back seat to what, probably, is still the closest the world has come to a Third World War…

The extremely tense situation between America and Russia highlighted at the start of this chapter came to a head between 16-28 October with a testing period, particularly on Wednesday 22 October. On the day Manchester United were playing the in-form Tottenham Hotspur away, Roy Cavanagh recalls he had other things on his mind!

'I had left school the previous June at the age of 15, quickly getting a job, as employment was readily available in those days. Although I was well into reading the newspapers in those days, I have to admit it was the back pages that drew my attention, although I was certainly aware of the rumbling world situation. Anyhow, on this particular Wednesday, it was common knowledge that the American's blockade of Cuba was going to be tested as the Russian fleet steamed that way. It was reported that by 3 pm English time, the two countries Navies would meet, with neither side seemingly willing to back down, the very real fear was one of them might push the dreaded nuclear button.

I was working in Salford and being the office junior, around that time, it was my role to climb the rickety wooden stairs to fill the required 20 or so cups of tea. I can still honestly tell you that I was coming back down those rickety stairs with this massive tray, full of cups of tea, I was thinking if that bomb goes off what a way to go!'

Luckily, there was a turning of the Russian ships, and over the next six days, the two countries came to a satisfactory conclusion of what, to this day, has been one of the most worrying encounters in the world. So, with one massive problem sorted, what would Manchester United's trip to Tottenham bring? The answer was an emphatic 6-2 defeat! Tottenham were a brilliant free-flowing side, highlighted by the magnificent Jimmy Greaves who turned on the style and scored a hat-trick.

The result turned out to be the lowest point for Manchester United, and thankfully, after this debacle, the form finally picked up. Bobby Charlton, although seemingly marginalised by being played as an outside left, had returned to full fitness and a forward line of Giles, Quixall, Herd, Law and Charlton just had to click. 3-1 victories over West Ham United and First Vienna of Austria in an Old Trafford friendly, was eclipsed as United went to Ipswich Town and won 5-3 with Denis Law scoring four linking brilliantly with Charlton. The Ipswich Town manager was Alf Ramsey, and as recently Walter Winterbottom had left his post as the England manager, it was Ramsey who the FA would turn to as their next leader.

The following Saturday against Liverpool saw the Manchester United chairman Harold Hardman celebrate 50 years as player, director and chairman of Manchester United. The contribution of Harold Hardman to Manchester United is huge. A man who worked tirelessly for the club, through the gloomy days of the 1930s the glory days after the war in the late 1940s and through to the creation and delivery of one of football's greatest sides, the Busby Babes by 1958. He was at the helm as the clubs entire future needed steering through that terrible air crash, but as always, put the club first. Harold Hardman fought not just for Manchester United but for football.

Hardman had also been an outstanding amateur footballer at the turn of the century, appearing in two FA Cup Finals for Everton, winning one and losing the other, and winning a Gold Medal for the Great Britain Olympic football team in the 1908 games in London. For modern-day United fans, imagine somebody the total opposite of the Glazers leading Manchester United, and you would find Harold Hardman.

The match against Liverpool was the first time since 1953 that the two sides had met in a league fixture, as under the leadership of the charismatic Bill Shankly, Liverpool had just returned from the wilderness of the Second Division. The atmosphere when the two Northern powerhouses met was so different from that of today, that unless you were around at the time, you would not believe. You could change ends at half-time passing the opposition fans on the way, even stand next to them and give your point of view! Those there in November 1962 witnessed a marvellous match, a Johnny Giles goal in the last-minute equalising the scores at 3-3.

United's form continued to improve, coming back from 2-0 down at Wolverhampton Wanderers to win 3-2 with another two goals from Denis Law, a 1-1 draw at Bramall Lane, still home at that time not just of Sheffield United but also Yorkshire County Cricket Club with the cricket pitch going right over to where the present cantilever stand is. When Nottingham Forest were hammered 5-1 at Old Trafford with four of the forwards amongst the goals, Herd getting two, it truly seemed Manchester United had turned the corner. The only disturbing feature though was that the attendance at Old Trafford for this match was just 27,392, despite full houses being seen at away matches.

The new glamour boy of football, Denis Law, got married in the week before the next fixture away at West Bromwich Albion. The honeymoon was put on hold, but whether it was a reaction to the wedding celebrations or not, United's undefeated run came to an end when they lost 3-0. There was, however, a very bizarre incident in this match involving Denis Law and the referee Gilbert Pullin. Denis reported to Matt Busby that Pullin had been taunting him with comments such as, *'Oh you clever so and so, you cannot play as well as you think you can'* Law and Busby decided to report the referee who was then severely censured. He did not take it all well and promptly resigned! Denis Law reflected in later years that after that, he was always treated harshly by the authorities and seemed to get large suspensions after being sent-off. Wags amongst the United fans though thought Denis got sent off near Christmas, so he was able to spend the New Year back in

Aberdeen!

Now well into December, the weather was going to have a major say, not just in football but for the whole country as one of the worst winters ever to hit these islands arrived. Towards the end of December, a lot of lower league fixtures had been postponed due to very heavy rain, and then around Christmas, a big freeze enveloped Britain which decimated the Football League. Indeed, from the evening of 23 December, there was not a frost-free night in Britain until 5 March 1963! United played on the Boxing Day of 1962 at Fulham, winning 1-0 and continuing the much-improved form since the return of Bobby Charlton and his growing partnership with Denis Law. They would not play an official fixture again until 23 February 1963.

There was no such thing as under soil heating in those days, clubs resorted to braziers to try to thaw their grounds and covering the pitch with loads of straw on top of tarpaulin sheets. For the general public, life was also very difficult with frozen roads, and as many people still got around on foot, many a slip! Due to the many postponements, the Pools Companies quickly reacting to the loss of income by creating a Pools Panel. The panel would meet on Friday night at a hotel and then, as games were cancelled, decide on the result they thought it would have been, a home, away or draw so that the dream of winning a lot of money was still there for the expectant public. Their first panel members included recently retired Tom Finney and former referee Arthur Ellis, who in later life became famous on the 'It's a Knockout' show on television. With the advent of the national lottery and other forms of gambling, the football pools are no longer such a prominent feature of everyday life.

The big freeze meant that Manchester United had seven consecutive Saturday fixtures called off. There was an amusing story doing the rounds about Denis Law and Matt Busby. In each of those seven matches, Manchester United were awarded a victory by the pools panel and Denis Law was alleged to say one Monday that he was going to ask the boss for the win bonus they were deprived of! When he arrived at the great man's door the conversation went like this;

'Morning Denis, what can I do for you?'

'Well boss, we have had seven wins according to the pools panel, and I was asking were we entitled to a win bonus?!'

'Aye, that seems a good idea Denis, but you were bloody dropped for those games so go away.'

During this extended break, United did get a couple of friendlies in over in Southern Ireland where the weather was more of heavy rain than snow and ice. During this time, Matt Busby decided that one of the still missing elements for what was quite a star-studded side on paper was a classy, creative wing-half. The man chosen was another Scot, somebody still loved by supporters 56 years on, Pat Crerand then of Glasgow Celtic. Signed for £55,000, while Pat had a relative lack of speed (ok he was slow!) and a dodgy temperament (ok he could look after himself!) he had an ability to pass the ball that was unsurpassed at Old Trafford until the Ginger Prince Paul Scholes joined 30 years later. Would Crerand be that link to make Manchester United great again, five years after Munich?

After getting a couple of draws as the fixtures started again, at home to Blackpool and away at Blackburn Rovers, the attention of all at Old Trafford turned to the FA Cup. The third round had paired Manchester United at home to the second division Huddersfield Town and was originally due to have been played on Saturday 5 January 1963; the match finally took place on Monday 4th March. Because of all the postponements, there was a severe fixture backlog. Incredibly thanks to the marvellous form Manchester United showed in the cup, they would be in the semi-final by the end of March! Roy Cavanagh recalls the start of an intense sequence of games.

The visit of Huddersfield gave me a chance to see one of my all-time heroes, goalkeeper Ray Wood who had been a massive part of the Busby Babes success, only being replaced as their goalkeeper a couple of months before the Munich disaster when Harry Gregg had joined on a record fee from Doncaster Rovers. Sadly, for Ray, he was not able to keep Denis Law at bay as Denis, himself a former Huddersfield Town player, helped himself to a hat-trick as United strolled through to round four with a 5-0 victory. This made it 16 goals in 24 matches for Denis, who was really justifying his enormous fee, looking every inch a superstar.'

A much harder tie awaited the following Monday night when Aston Villa visited Old Trafford, but a single Albert Quixall goal gave United some revenge for their heart-breaking 2-1 FA Cup Final defeat of 1957 by Villa in which the horrific injury Ray Wood suffered after only six minutes meant that Manchester United played virtually all the final with ten men.

Incredibly, only 12 days after the third-round tie, Manchester United were playing another second division side, Chelsea at Old Trafford in the fifth round. Chelsea, managed by Tommy Docherty, were starting to make a name for themselves as their young side were playing attractive football. A close match saw United get through again by a single goal, this time 2-1 with Albert Quixall continuing his record of scoring in all the rounds so far. Interestingly, in the match programme for this match, it reflected on the forthcoming England v Scotland match at Wembley, suggesting that the Scotland side was far superior to the English team having such as Law and Crerand from United and Dave MacKay, Bill Brown and John White of Tottenham Hotspur amongst their 11. Those last three had just been to Old Trafford on the Saturday between the Huddersfield and Aston Villa cup ties and helped beat United 2-0 to end United's decent run of league form. In the end, it was a correct assumption that Scotland would beat

England as they won 2-1 at the 'new' Wembley Stadium which had just had full cover around the ground installed costing £750,000. Forty years on, a totally 'new' Wembley would cost £750 million!

At the end of March 1963, Manchester United would play their fourth FA Cup tie of the month and qualify for the FA Cup semi-final. Their sixth-round tie would take them away from Old Trafford for the first time in this cup run, away to third division Coventry City, managed by the man who had fought so hard for footballers over the maximum wage, Jimmy Hill. Coventry were on the crest of a wave unbeaten in 22 matches and having a record Highfield Road crowd of 44,000 urging them on. They also had the advantage of it chucking it down, so much so that the pitch was a complete mud bath. Pre-match the crowd had Ken Dodd providing the entertainment, it did not have the makings of a promising day, which got worse as Coventry went 1-0 up inside the first ten minutes. Bobby Charlton, though, had a great match scoring two goals with Albert Quixall again getting a goal and putting United into the semi-finals.

Having got a semi-final to look forward to, it seemed Manchester United took their eye completely off their league position. Dangerously so, and by the end of April, they would be fully aware of how precarious their league situation was. A total of eight league games were played, two wins, two draws and four defeats leaving the side fighting with Birmingham City and local neighbours Manchester City for the dubious privilege of joining the seemingly doomed Leyton Orient into the second division.

Villa Park always holds a special place in Manchester United supporter's hearts and the 27 April 1963 only confirmed that as that man Denis Law scored the only goal against second division Southampton. Playing in all white as both clubs had to change colours in those days in the FA Cup when there was a clash, surely this victory would provide the impetus to clear any relegation fears?

Three defeats in the next four matches, including against fellow strugglers Birmingham City, left that threat starkly on the table. It also produced one of the most important and controversial Manchester derby matches for over 40 years. City would have the home advantage. Roy Cavanagh made the journey to Moss Side and recalls that very tense night.

'A packed Maine Road, myself included, saw Alex Harley put City one-nil up early on, and in all honesty control the match. For some reason, the United players were playing as though it was just another game, and Wembley was only just over a week away. I was in the old Platt Lane stand and in the second half United were playing towards the open scoreboard end in those days at Maine Road, but from even a distance it seemed a strange decision for the City keeper Harry Dowd to make with only five minutes left. He seemed to chase Denis Law to the edge of the penalty area, going away from goal when Denis seemed to fall over Dowd's outstretched arm. Albert Quixall was one of the best penalty takers I have seen, and he slotted home the goal which kept United

up and put City down.'

Albert Quixall was once Manchester United's record signing and called the 'Golden Boy' of English football, his late penalty covered his fee and enhanced his reputation. Albert recalled that penalty a few years later.

'A defeat for either side meant relegation, so you can imagine my feelings when Denis won us a penalty with only five minutes to go. It was the only time in my career that I felt apprehensive about taking a penalty, but luckily, it went in, and we stayed up.'

The following morning's Daily Mirror reported on the controversial game. Fortunately, perhaps for a certain recent signing from Scotland, there were no tunnel-cams in those days.

'A scuffle in the tunnel at half-time between a player from either side, three men booked, a succession of petty fouls. This was the background of bubbling violence to a Derby game that was climaxed six minutes from time with a hotly disputed penalty. .... The penalty came when City keeper Dowd became tangled with Denis Law. Referee George McCabe awarded the penalty without hesitation, although Dowd was KO'd in the incident.......... The tunnel incident was out of my view – but photographers who were on the spot within seconds – reported that Wagstaffe had to be helped to the dressing room.'

Had United lost they would have been a point behind City with just one match left. United went on to win their remaining fixture 3-1 at home to Johnny Carey's already relegated Orient. The final league table looked like this.

Pos	Team	Pld	F	A	GD	Pts
19	Manchester United	42	67	81	−14	34
20	Birmingham City	42	63	90	−27	33
21	Manchester City	42	58	102	−44	31
22	Leyton Orient	42	37	81	−44	21

With their position in the First Division secured, Saturday 25 May 1963 marked the start of Manchester United's glory years of the 1960s. A packed, sweltering Wembley Stadium saw the individual stars of United at last play as a team to defeat the team who had been one of the best all season, Leicester City. Let us hear from one of the players on the day, Albert Quixall.

'Every footballer knew then that the FA Cup was the biggest day of their career especially if you win! We stayed at a lovely hotel in Weybridge, and our preparations were excellent. At our team talk, Matt Busby told us to go out and enjoy ourselves and not get ruffled, play the ball about across the Wembley turf and make Leicester do the running. As it turned out, it was a much easier match than we could have imagined, just like a practice match really. After the first five minutes you could sense it was our day; all the

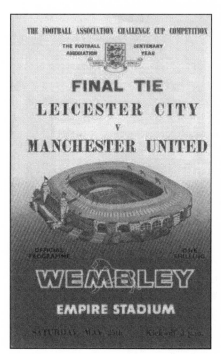

THE FOOTBALL ASSOCIATION CHALLENGE CUP COMPETITION

THE FOOTBALL ASSOCIATION · CENTENARY YEAR

FINAL TIE

LEICESTER CITY

V

MANCHESTER UNITED

OFFICIAL PROGRAMME · ONE SHILLING

WEMBLEY

EMPIRE STADIUM

SATURDAY, MAY 25th · Kick-off 3 p.m.

team were on top of their game. Denis Law scored a marvellous goal after 15 minutes, and then David Herd made it 2-0 before half time. Even though Leicester pulled a goal back, David Herd scored his second, and our third to give us the cup.'

The Manchester United side who won the club's first FA Cup since 1948, and the first trophy since 1957 was; Gaskell, Dunne, Cantwell (Capt.), Crerand, Foulkes, Setters, Giles, Quixall, Herd, Law and Charlton.

1962/63 was a season which had seen Denis Law and Pat Crerand join Manchester United, Everton win the Football League title, the threat of the Third World War, the worst winter in living memory, the creation of the Pools Panel, and also seen Manchester United nearly relegated AND win the FA Cup. They would also be back in European football competition…

.

Chapter Five

EUROPEAN RETURN

1963-64

During the summer break on 8 August 1963, the Great Train Robbery occurred with goods worth £2.6 million stolen from a Royal Mail train heading from Glasgow to London as it passed through Buckinghamshire. Two years later one of the convicted robbers, Ronnie Biggs, escaped from Wandsworth, eventually going on to live in Rio de Janeiro.

The Conservative Party had been in government since Winston Churchill was elected Prime Minister in 1951. Their current leader, Harold Macmillan, had been Prime Minister since 1957. The scandals that rocked his government changed the political and social landscape of Britain forever, eventually bringing another Harold to power. Macmillan would remain Prime Minister until October 1963. The year had started badly for Macmillan, as in January Charles de Gaulle, the French leader had said 'Non' to Britain's application to join the Common Market, as it was known before it became the European Union (and any sign of the word Brexit!).

Things went from bad to worse for Macmillan as his party became engulfed in sex and espionage scandals. In January double agent Kim Philby left his post in Beirut and defected to the Soviet Union. The ramifications of this didn't surface until later in the year. In early June, John Profumo Secretary of State for War resigned after he was found to have misled parliament over his relationship with Christine Keeler. Profumo had met Keeler at a party organised by osteopath and socialite Christopher Ward. Ward's circle included such figures as Lord Astor, whose ancestral home of Cliveden was used to host parties. The circle also included Russian Military attaché and known intelligence officer, Yevgeny Ivanov. The combination of sex and spying proved irresistible to the press which feasted upon the story. The police began to investigate Ward who, in many ways became the scapegoat. He was convicted of living off immoral earnings but died of an overdose before the verdict was announced. Within a month Kim Philby was revealed to be the 'The Third Man' in a spy scandal that had involved the 1951 defection to the Soviet Union of MI6 agents, Guy Burgess and Donald Maclean. It was revealed that Philby had tipped the pair off. The magnitude of the scandal can only be understood by the fact that Philby was for many years MI6's anti-Soviet section. Labour backbenchers pursued Harold Macmillan who had himself approved Philby's security clearance when he had been the Foreign Secretary back in 1956. When the economy started to have difficulties by October 1963, it was the final straw for Macmillan, who also had health issues at the time, and he resigned. Macmillan was replaced as Prime Minister, much to the surprise of many in the country, by Alec Douglas-Home, old Etonian and the epitome of a toff.

An interesting reflection on those changing times is that, while a sex scandal eventually did for his Premiership, but not his Government, Macmillan's wife, Dorothy, had been having an affair for over 30 years with Conservative Politician Bob Boothby, later Lord Boothby. He was a larger than life character, often rumoured to be involved with the Kray twins due to his sexual inclinations. It was widely thought that Macmillan's daughter had been fathered by Boothby. In a striking example of the difference between reporting in the 1960s and 2019, none of this was printed, at the time. A remarkable difference to today when social media has the news online quicker than official news information sources. In many ways, the Profumo Affair marked the beginning of that change.

It wasn't just politics that would change forever during the 63-64 season. Popular music witnessed a revolution too. Thus far the charts in the 1960s had been dominated by Elvis Presley who had had nine number-one singles. In 1963 he topped the charts for a solitary week, the Beatles hit number one in May 1963 with *From Me to You* and stayed there for the next seven weeks. *She Loves You* topped the charts for six weeks, and *I Wanna Hold Your Hand* for five. It wasn't just the Beatles though. The start of the year it was Cliff Richard and the Shadows that led the way, but once the Beatles arrived Gerry & the Pacemakers, The Searchers, Billy J Kramer and the Tremeloes all made it to the top. British Pop music, with its own youth culture, had arrived. Rock n Roll wasn't about to go quietly though. The Spring of 1964 saw Mods & Rockers clash at Clacton and Brighton beaches. Youth culture had arrived and with it a sense of rebellion. It wouldn't be too long before this was reflected on the football terraces too, where fans of opposing sides had previously been happy to mingle…

For Manchester United, the extremely poor league form of the previous season, when 19th position was most definitely Matt Busby's lowest ever league place, was balanced with a sense of optimism generated by their FA Cup victory. There were no major signings, and Matt Busby seemed prepared to put his faith in the Manchester United side which had finally come good and won the FA Cup for the first time since 1948. In doing so, he could gain extra confidence from the ability of the promising young players that he knew would come through to challenge his established side.

Pre-season United were brought down to earth after their Wembley heroics when a Glasgow select side beat them 2-1. A 1-1 draw with German side Eintracht Frankfurt followed a match in which Noel Cantwell was sent off. These games were the prelude to the Charity Shield meeting with the 1963 League Champions, Everton. In those times the match was played at the home of the League Champions, and so it was off to a packed Goodison Park. One interesting note was that United played in all white, which was due to the continuing uptake of televisions in more and more homes. Television still only provided black and white pictures, and it was decided that the United players in an all-white kit would be easier to pick out. Well, they would be seen running towards their own goal for most of the match as Everton, who were a super side, won easily by a margin of 4-0 and United were lucky to get nil!

This was enough for Busby. He was not prepared to have another season of league football as poor as the previous one and decided that the senior players needed a real shakeup. For one of the players, Johnny Giles, it became a shakeout. He was not happy at being dropped, feeling he was not being played in his best position, which Johnny felt was inside-forward. Matt Busby though had spent a lot of money on Albert Quixall, and his preference for Quixall meant Johnny Giles was pushed to outside-right. When push came to shove Busby was always prepared to act quickly, within a week Giles was transferred to Leeds United. Leeds manager Don Revie felt this was a real coup that would prove decisive in their attempts to gain promotion back to the First Division. Revie would be proved right, as Johnny Giles went on to become one of the very few that have left Old Trafford and flourished.

The first league fixture was at Hillsborough, home of Sheffield Wednesday, and as well as Giles, David Gaskell, David Herd and ironically Albert Quixall were all dropped to be replaced by Harry Gregg, David Sadler and Phil Chisnall respectively, with Ian Moir coming in for Giles. The three outfield players were youngsters, and they immediately gave the club a lift as the team drew 3-3 thanks to a goal from Moir and two from Bobby Charlton.

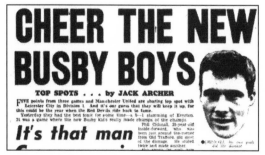

When Denis Law got back into his goal-scoring mood and scored both goals in a 2-0 home victory against Ipswich Town, a quick return match with champions Everton at Old Trafford, this time a league fixture, was eagerly looked forward to. Everton were a fine side, having the backing of the Littlewoods Pools magnate John Moores, and his managers had spent his money wisely. Alex Parker, Jimmy Gabriel, Alex Scott and Alex Young were all big-money signings from Scotland, while Tony Kay, Dennis Stevens and Roy Vernon were expensive purchases from English clubs. The winning of the First Division and the dismantling of United in the Charity Shield was already starting to repay the investment, but Old Trafford witnessed the re-birth of Manchester United when Everton arrived on 31 August 1963 as United won 5-1. The trio of young homegrown forwards in Ian Moir, Phil Chisnall and David Sadler brought pace and skill while the other two forwards, another homegrown in Bobby Charlton and the record signing Denis Law supplied the real class and skill to send Everton home down the East Lancashire road with a heavy defeat.

An incredible 7-2 away victory at Ipswich Town, completing a quick double over a side who were recent champions, saw four goals from Denis Law and Manchester United at the top of the league. United were still top six matches later in mid-September as West Bromwich Albion arrived at Old Trafford for a match that has gone down in the history of Manchester United. The match was the day that a 17-year-old Northern Irish lad called George Best made his debut. George had first come to Old Trafford in July 1961 as he left school in Belfast, two days later he was on his way back to Belfast due to homesickness! Matt Busby quickly heard about this and a phone call to George's father, Dick asking George to return would confirm the arrival of a player who would become one of the greatest footballers in the world...

It must have seemed a long first season for George as he flipped between the 'A' and 'B' teams, although he did get his first Old Trafford appearance in the FA Youth Cup team in the previous 1962-63 season before making his reserve debut at the start of this 1963-64 season. He had not made many appearances at reserve level before he was flung into first-team action due to an injury to Ian Moir. The match programme for the West Bromwich Albion match has Moir at number seven, but an announcement to the crowd confirmed a team change - it would be George Best playing number seven. A crowd of 50,453 witnessed the debut, Roy Cavanagh amongst them.

This was the first real sight of George for most of the United fans, and I can still remember this very slim, dark-haired young lad, only a year older than me, taking on this grizzled left full-back, Graham Williams, himself a Wales full international. It soon became apparent to all that the young lad had talent, loads of it in fact. He seemed to have his head tilted on his shoulder, beat a man either side, and was not afraid to have a shot at goal. If he was caught in a tackle, fair or otherwise, he just got up and left them for dead the next time. George helped United win the game 1-0 thanks to a goal from his mate, young centre forward David Sadler. United stayed clear at the top of the table after seven undefeated matches.'

'For the next three months I would regularly see George on a Tuesday or a Thursday night at the new sensation of ten pin bowling where a new alley near the Lancashire County Cricket Club ground a short walk from the Old Trafford football stadium had opened. He had dropped back to the reserves after his debut but would be back to stay at

Christmas 1963. George will appear throughout this decade, suffice to say he developed into the greatest footballer I ever saw.'

As his programme above shows, Roy Cavanagh was paying attention to the team announcements made over the tannoy. George Best had made his debut in place of Moir, and Nobby Stiles had replaced Denis Law. The report in Monday's Birmingham Post showed that their reporter, Cyril Chapman, had been less observant! Cyril reported on the tussle between United's number 7 and the West Brom full-back Graham Williams. Little did he realise he was witnessing the debut of one of the greatest players that ever lived.

'A huge crowd, come mainly to see United consolidate their position at the top of the First Division, had a long time to wait for the first golden moment for the winning goal did not come until half-way through the second-half. Little patience was shown during the waiting period. The Manchester inefficiencies were as roundly criticised as Albion's temerity in daring to check the crowd's red-shirted darlings as they came down to goal.

Chief target was left-back Graham Williams who naturally gave new United youngster MOIR no more consideration as he would have done an experienced player. The Albion player cheerfully blew kisses to the crowd as he continued with a defensive display which was extremely encouraging to Albion in their more difficult moments.'

There has never been a better judge of a young player than Matt Busby. He had seen the amazing talent that George and one or two other young players of his generation possessed when he reported, *'We have been particularly fortunate over the years with the talent we have produced because we firmly believe in a progressive youth policy and although it can be costly, it is also very rewarding. Already this season two 17-year-olds have had the taste of First Division football – centre-forward David Sadler and Belfast born winger George Best. These two youngsters obviously have a big future in football'.* Prophetic words from the great Manchester United manager…

Tuesday 15 October 1963 marked the return of European football to Old Trafford when Manchester United played their 2nd leg Cup Winners Cup tie against the Dutch cup winners, Willem 11. The first leg had been a 1-1 draw in a game switched from Willem's stadium to the larger Feyenoord stadium in Rotterdam. David Herd scored United's goal but was then sent off, but Old Trafford saw a different tie as a Denis Law hat-trick helped United to a 6-1 victory.

BUSBY BABES

MARK PEARSON

Youngsters establishing themselves in the first-team inevitably had consequences for some of the older players. In October 1963, another of the players who had played in the first match of the 1960s, Mark Pearson, left Manchester United. Mark was an extremely gifted inside-left who at 17 was a real star in the youth sides, linking brilliantly with centre-forward Alex Dawson. He was already well in the minds of Matt Busby and Jimmy Murphy before Munich, indeed, travelled with the side as 12th man for the famous match against Arsenal played on the Saturday before the air crash. That crash precipitated his debut in the first game after Munich, the 5th round FA Cup tie against Sheffield Wednesday at Old Trafford. Sheffield was Mark's place of birth, and it would be to the Wednesday that he was transferred in October 1963. Nicknamed 'Pancho' due to his Mexican looks with long sideburns he was a very creative inside-forward, though it has to be said that he knew how to protect himself on the field,

In November 1963 the grounds that would stage matches for the 1966 world cup finals in England were named with Old Trafford one of the eight allotted grounds. November 1963 would see two massive matches at Old Trafford against Tottenham Hotspur, and Liverpool played against the background of memorable events close to home and dramatically on the world stage.

Saturday 9th November 1963 saw two of those events take place. At Old Trafford, Manchester United entertained Tottenham Hotspur in a top of the table match, only three weeks before they were due to meet in the next round of the European Cup Winners Cup over two legs. Denis Law was still in majestic form and scored a hat trick as United beat the excellent Tottenham Hotspur side 4-1 to gain some psychological advantage for the forthcoming European games. Less than four miles away that day saw the closure of the Manchester Horse Racing course.

Like Manchester Docks, Manchester Racecourse was in fact located in Salford, at Castle Irwell. Racing had been held there since the 1700s. For a period, the racing had been moved to New Barns in Weaste but had moved back to Castle Irwell in 1898. The racecourse, which held the first-ever evening meeting in 1951 was the home to the Lancashire Oaks (now held at Haydock) and the last big handicap of the flat season – the November Handicap (now held at Doncaster.) Structural problems with the main stand began to appear by the 1960s, and so one of the country's first concrete cantilever stands was built enabling the course to become the first with private viewing boxes. Sadly, though the costs of the building of the stand created financial problems and on 9 November 1963, it's last ever meeting took place. A crowd of 57,513 crammed into Old Trafford for the Tottenham match but just down the road in Salford over 20,000 witnessed Lester Piggott win the final race at the track, fittingly named the Goodbye Consolation Plate.

The transfer of Mark Pearson opened up the arrival of Wales inside-forward Graham Moore from Chelsea, and he made his debut in the Tottenham match, a signing which must have raised eyebrows across the Pennines for Johnny Giles. Perhaps Matt Busby was already realising that it might have been hasty to let him go to Leeds United. This was emphasised the week after when United suffered a shock 4-0 defeat away at Aston Villa, although the sending off of Denis Law did not help matters!

The run-up to the following Saturday's match against Liverpool at Old Trafford would feature events of national and international significance. The world was rocked by the assassination of the American President John F. Kennedy on 22 November 1963. Closer to home, but certainly nationally and internationally significant was the development of Beatlemania. That week Roy Cavanagh would see the Beatles play a concert in Manchester. Here he reflects on the significance of both events.

'Music was certainly playing a bigger part in the lives of young people now, with groups from Liverpool and Manchester bringing their distinctive sounds to people. At the beginning of November, a Liverpool group called Gerry & the Pacemakers had a number one record called 'You'll never walk alone' a song which of course still resonates today, while when the chance to see The Beatles came I was off to what was then the ABC cinema in Ardwick Green Manchester. The concert was on Wednesday 20 November with the sound of loads of girls screaming as the group appeared, and indeed, while they performed all their songs.

Forty-Eight hours later I was outside Lewis's arcade in Piccadilly Manchester waiting for somebody, when the big newsreel opposite confirmed the news that President John F. Kennedy had indeed been assassinated in Dallas, Texas. This would be another "where were you moment" for me for the rest of my life, as Kennedy, a figure of the times, with his relative youth, good looks and persuasive talk had seemed the bright young thing to lead the world never mind America.

Life goes on of course, and a packed Old Trafford the following day saw the visit of Liverpool, riding high near the top of the table with United. The game decided by a goal from the Liverpool captain, Ronnie Yeats from a corner, during which he also collided heavily with United's goalkeeper Harry Gregg causing the popular Irishman to suffer yet another serious injury. Centre-forward David Herd had to go in goal and United were not only being a goal down but also a man as there was still no substitutes in those days. It certainly brought the end of a truly memorable week for me; one I still recall 56 years on.'

In the programme for the visit of Liverpool was an amazing story from the respected journalist Harry Ditton of the News of the World who reported that he had learnt that the Football Association were considering creating an international league covering 25 European countries. Now, this was incredible, because only eight years earlier, the Football League had been against clubs entering the new European Cup, actually denying Chelsea the first opportunity to do so. Matt Busby, of course, had rejected that 'advice' and Manchester United entered the 1956-57 European Cup, which would cause years of serious conflict between the Football League, particularly their Secretary Alan Hardaker, and Manchester United.

Over the past two seasons, just as United were about to play Arsenal, fog had descended over Old Trafford causing the postponement of the matches. It had also happened when Tottenham Hotspur had been due to play at Old Trafford in their double season in 1961. Well, in November 1963 it was the fog of North London which had its revenge and caused a Manchester United away match to be cancelled just as kick-off was about to take place. The postponed match was for the European Cup Winners Cup first-leg tie at Tottenham Hotspur with the teams virtually ready to start the game. Ronnie Briggs was again thrown into the fray due to a serious injury to Harry Gregg, but the delay enabled David Gaskell to return from injury the following Saturday for the away match at Sheffield United.

While United won in Sheffield 2-1 thanks to another two-goal salvo from Denis Law which kept them near the top of the table, it was a very different story when the European tie took place the following week in London. Tottenham, with Jimmy Greaves like Denis Law, a truly world-class forward, were determined to defend the European trophy they had won the previous May. Though United played well on the night a late, second Tottenham goal meant a very difficult second-leg at Old Trafford for Manchester United.

Stoke City had been promoted the previous season successfully pursuing a policy of recruiting famous footballers either coming to an end of their career or needing a new challenge. When they arrived at Old Trafford, their line-up included ex-United favourite Dennis Viollet, former Burnley magician Jimmy McIlroy, Peter Dobing the former Blackburn Rovers and Manchester City favourite AND the legendary Stanley Matthews, back at the club he had started his career many years ago. Indeed, Stanley was 48 years old as he took his place on the right-wing at Old Trafford. It was, however, yet another virtuoso performance by United's Denis Law which stole the show from Stoke's star-studded side as he scored four goals in United's 5-2 victory.

United were now two points off the top of the table, but then news reached them that for his sending off at Aston Villa, Denis Law was to get a four-week suspension, note time in those days as opposed to matches missed. At the time suspensions included all competitions and so it meant Denis was suspended for the vital second-leg of the European Cup Winners Cup tie at Old Trafford against Tottenham Hotspur.

A real glamour night at Old Trafford saw a magnificent football match, tinged with tragedy as Tottenham's all-action left-half, Dave MacKay suffered a broken leg in a collision with United's Noel Cantwell. David Herd and Bobby Charlton stepped up to the plate for United in this game, both scoring twice which, despite a goal from Jimmy Greaves, meant a magnificent 4-1 victory, 4-3 on aggregate for Manchester United against the current holders of the Cup Winners Cup.

With Christmas coming up, United near the top of the table, into the quarter-finals of a major European competition and the draw for the FA Cup about to take place things looked rosy for Manchester United. Never count your chickens! Two away defeats, hammerings really, 4-0 at Everton and 6-1 at Burnley on Boxing Day were a real wake-up call as the loss of Denis Law kicked in. The Burnley defeat was particularly embarrassing, with another sending off, this time Pat Crerand, not helping matters. One of the architects of the Burnley victory was their young outside-right Willie Morgan who recalled in an interview with Roy Cavanagh how he saw the match.

'Manchester United came to Turf Moor without the suspended Denis Law and met a Burnley team right up for the match. We turned them over 6-1, and Pat Crerand got sent off as well, I felt it was one of my best ever games for Burnley, I scored twice and made the other four, all scored by Andy Lochhead, who was a great centre forward for a winger to aim at. Noel Cantwell was marking me that day, and I turned him inside out, so much so he told me what he was going to do to me in the return a day or so later if he caught me, which he did!'

That return came at Old Trafford and saw Matt Busby make big decisions. He called young George Best back from his Christmas holiday in Belfast for his second league game and brought in at outside-right a young lad who was a month off his 17th birthday, Willie Anderson. The pair had starred recently for the FA Youth Cup side when they had beat Barrow by the exceptional score of 14-1 with George scoring a hat-trick against a side which included a young Emlyn Hughes, later of course to captain Liverpool and England. The changes made an immediate difference as Willie Morgan again recalled.

'This was the game George Best was put back into the side, only this time as outside-left opposite myself. George would score his first Manchester United goal and had a great game as they hammered us 5-1. I had started off as I did at Turf Moor a couple of days before giving Noel Cantwell a hard time, only this time he caught me, and there was such an almighty wallop, and I landed in the dugouts! I didn't enjoy that match!'

Keeping the young players in the side, Manchester United had cup success at Southampton winning 3-2, before suffering a surprising home defeat to Birmingham City. Then a visit to West Bromwich Albion saw a famous day in the history of Manchester United. This was the game that what became known as the 'Holy Trinity' of Bobby Charlton, Denis Law and George Best would all appear in the same Manchester United side for the first time. Fittingly, all three would score as well, Denis getting two as United won 4-1.

As Manchester United went into February 1964, they were in 6th position in the league, in the 5th round of the FA Cup after overcoming Bristol Rovers 4-1 at Old Trafford, and the quarter-finals of the European Cup Winners Cup. Denis Law was a pivotal part of this progress, his hat trick against Bristol Rovers was his fifth of the season and included his 26th goal in all fixtures.

The season was coming to the boil for United, and now came the crux – well placed in the league and with quarter-final ties in both cup competitions, against Sunderland in the FA Cup and home to Sporting Lisbon in the Cup Winners Cup. When the Portuguese cup holders Sporting Lisbon appeared at Old Trafford in their iconic green and white shirts, they ran straight into another virtuoso display from Denis Law. Yet another hat-trick, including two penalties, gave United a great opportunity to progress. The match programme informed fans that you could fly to

Lisbon for the return match for £33 guineas which also included a hotel stopover!

Things were looking up for United. Fighting on three fronts and in great form, surely at least one trophy would be coming to Old Trafford at the end of the season? What followed next was an unprecedented example of fixture congestion when in March Manchester United had to play ten vital games in just 26 days, in an era before substitutes and the development of the squad game. It is a widely accepted maxim nowadays that modern players are mollycoddled in comparison to the valiant players of old who would play game after game with no complaint. There may be truth in this, but players are only human, and in the end, something had to give for United. In the event, the trip to Lisbon had to be postponed, in those days European matches took second place to domestic football, and as United's FA Cup quarter-final match with Sunderland ended 3-3, the replay had to be completed before the second-leg in Lisbon. As was the custom then, both sides had to change colours, so United wore all-white for a series of matches which would go into Manchester United's FA Cup history.

Sunderland were chasing promotion to the first division and in their centre-half and captain, Charlie Hurley, they had one of the real characters of the game. In a pulsating match, before a packed-out crowd, incredibly Sunderland led, and deservedly, 3-1 with only five minutes to go. The holders looked down and out, but two late goals levelled the scores at 3-3 leading to a Roker Park replay, necessitating the cancellation of the Sporting Lisbon 2nd leg tie.

Manchester United, therefore, went to the North East instead of Lisbon and the sights that greeted them had to be seen to be believed. Roker Park was a massive ground in those days, holding 70,000 who easily filled the ground with what seemed like many thousands more as talk of gates being broken down, with some distressing scenes, as more people wanted to see the match. Again, Sunderland dictated the progress of the game, leading 1-0 before an equaliser took the match into extra time, with yet another United equaliser ending the match at 2-2.

In between what would be a third match to settle matters for a semi-final spot, United went to West Ham United to play a league fixture, which had extra significance as the winners of the United v Sunderland tie would play West Ham at Hillsborough the following Saturday. Roy Cavanagh recalls the times.

'I travelled to London on the 11.55pm Friday night train from Piccadilly Station arriving in Euston at 6.30am, interspersed with stopping at sidings, no heating on a very long, cold journey. Incidentally, Manchester Piccadilly had been renamed in 1960 from London Road Station. Back in 1964, on arrival in London, it was breakfast at Joe Lyon's corner house, before a brief tour of the capital on my first-time visit, before arriving at Upton Park in London's East End. When the teams were announced, it seemed to be a wasted journey as Matt Busby made wholesale changes with all the cup ties going on, and only included goalkeeper David Gaskell and wing-half Pat Crerand from his regular side, against what was a full-strength West Ham, including Bobby Moore, Martin Peters and Geoff Hurst.

Showing the unpredictability of the game, United won comfortably 2-0, giving them a great incentive to beat Sunderland on the Monday night's second replay. That match was to be played at Leeds Road, home of Huddersfield Town. This time I went by coach, to witness a match in front of another capacity crowd of 55,000, with thousands yet again locked out. When Sunderland again took the lead, it seemed they were favourites, but United, led by Denis Law in majestic form, not only equalised but went on in the second-half to win 5-1! It would be them who went to Sheffield for yet another semi-final.'

With Manchester United reverting to their full side it seemed they would be strong favourites, but for United at least the match was literally a damp squib. Torrential rain turned Hillsborough into a quagmire, and amazingly the referee allowed the match to take place. With United having to go to Lisbon the following Wednesday it makes you wonder whether that was the reason the game was played, but it was more than a leveller, and West Ham adapted far better to go through to Wembley as 3-1 victors.

Out of one cup, the disasters continued when the second leg of the European Cup Winners Cup took place in Lisbon against Sporting, which caused what is still the worst ever European defeat for Manchester United. A 5-0 scoreline put Sporting through 6-4 on aggregate. In later years, Pat Crerand would recall that this left Matt Busby in the angriest mood the players had ever seen. That they could return to England and play Tottenham Hotspur in London and win 3-2 showed how much they had moved on from the previous season, however, and still left United in with the chance of the title at least.

The fact that games had piled up after the various replays and trips to Europe, the sheer weight of matches took its toll, and a season-defining defeat at Liverpool would take the title to them.

Pos	Club	Pld	W	D	L	GF	GA	Pts
1	Liverpool	42	26	5	11	92	45	57
2	Manchester United	42	23	7	12	90	62	53
3	Everton	42	21	10	11	84	64	52

Despite the lack of silverware, United's progress to runners up position and their performances in the cup competitions was a huge improvement on previous seasons. The crowds were up too, with an average of 43,687 in the League and huge crowds in the cup competitions. The season had seen the emergence of George Best and the debut of the Holy Trinity. Of the three, it was Denis Law that was the key player. The impact that he had cannot be underestimated. The 'King' played 30 of the 42 league games, his suspension and a few knocks depriving United of his services for 12 games, but still scored 30 goals only two behind Dennis Viollet's club record. In the other 12 cup matches that he played Denis scored an incredible 16 goals, meaning a total of 46 goals in 42 matches!

Despite the improvement, Matt Busby wasn't satisfied. At the end of the season, he moved into the transfer market and made a very astute purchase in the Burnley winger John Connelly. Connelly was a fast, goal-scoring, experienced player and made a mouth-watering prospect for the following season of a forward line of, Connelly, Charlton. Herd, Law and Best.

Away from United, the season had ended on a mote of controversy as on Sunday 12 April 1964 the story broke that three footballers, Tony Kay (then of champions Everton), Peter Swan and David (Bronco) Layne both of Sheffield Wednesday were accused of betting offences on matches. They would be sent to prison for four months each on 26 January 1965 and banned for life from playing football. Two of the players, Kay and Swan had appeared for England in international matches.

There were other important activities at Old Trafford as the season drew to a close. Firstly, news that for the World Cup matches due to be played at Old Trafford in the summer of 1966, the stadium would undergo radical changes. The building of a cantilever stand was to commence at the end of this season; it would be 660 feet long, providing seating for 10,000 and covered standing for a further 10,000. The cantilever would reach 48 feet high at its front, obviously giving clear views instead of the obstructed views created by stanchions in traditional designs. Fittingly, the company that Roy Cavanagh worked for over 50 years, G&J Seddon (now known as Seddon) would build this stand, only the third such in England after those built at Scunthorpe and Sheffield Wednesday.

One of Manchester United's other sides, their FA Youth Cup team, had made excellent progress during the season and after beating local rivals City in the semi-final over two legs 8-4 on aggregate, they played Swindon Town in the final. Both sides had brilliant young leaders in George Best for United and Don Rogers for Swindon, and they both scored in the first-leg played before a full house in Swindon. Manchester United had developed a top-class side though and in the home leg at Old Trafford won 4-1 on the night with David Sadler scoring a hat trick. He, along with George Best, John Aston, and Jimmy Rimmer (unused substitute) would be in the European Cup-winning side four years on, while Bobby Noble, John Fitzpatrick, Willie Anderson and Albert Kinsey would all play first-team matches for Manchester United.

So, the season had ended trophyless, but great progress had been made. As a further reminder of this, May saw West Ham United win the FA Cup, and Sporting Lisbon win the European Cup Winners Cup, at least Manchester United had lost out to the eventual winners of those trophies. !964-65 promised much for the newly resurgent Manchester United.

Chapter Six

BACK AT THE TOP

1964-65

Politically and socially in the UK, the period covered by the 1964-65 season was less dramatic than the previous two seasons. If there had been any doubt that the changes that had occurred in society were permanent, those doubts were ended. On 15 October 1964, the Conservative Government under Alec Douglas-Home were defeated in the General Election by the Labour party under the leadership of Harold Wilson. The majority though was a miserly four seats, but Labour would fight through, before going to the country again in 1966. Harold Wilson was a most interesting man, widely regarded as The Queen's favourite Prime Minister over the many she has had during her long reign. Wilson, of course, had himself only succeeded Hugh Gaitskell as Labour leader when he had died suddenly in 1963. We will discuss Harold Wilson and his relationship with football more during the 1960s.

Internationally, the situation in Vietnam was causing mounting concern. Although Vietnam had been a troubled country since the Second World War, you could go back to the First World War when America was first asked to become involved in that country. By 1964, America's involvement was escalating rapidly. The conflict that followed for the next ten years, and the terrible loss of life, scarred American politics and life.

In Motor Racing, Englishman John Surtees, after winning four Motorcycle Grand Prix in the 1950s, won the Formula One version driving for Ferrari. A feat that has never been repeated and Surtees is a true great of the speed and danger of motorsports. 1964 also saw the emergence of an international superstar. A star who would become enmeshed in the controversy over Vietnam. A young Cassius Clay had sensationally defeated the champion Sonny Liston in Miami Beach, America. Clay, who had been 7/1 with the bookmakers, was then only 22. Although Clay was an Olympic light-heavyweight champion, the fearsome Liston was considered to be far too strong. In a sensational fight Clay eventually overpowered Liston, who did not come out for the seventh round. Sonny Liston had a very chequered life and career. He was the second oldest of his mother's 13 children, while his father had already had a further 12 children with his first wife. He would lose again to Clay in a later fight. As for Cassius Clay, he briefly became known as Cassius X, then very quickly Muhammad Ali with his famous announcement: *'Cassius Clay is a slave name. I didn't choose it, and I don't want it. I am Muhammad Ali, a free name – it means beloved of God, and I insist people use it when people speak to me'.* The rest is history; he would develop into a new phenomenon – a genuinely international sporting superstar, one of the most famous people in the world and perhaps the most famous sportsman of all time.

Since March 1964 youngsters had been able to listen to their favourite artists via pirate station Radio Caroline anchored off Felixstowe. The Beatles had been at the forefront of the change in popular music, but many more would follow. June 1964 would see the Rolling Stones have their first number-one single 'It's All Over Now'. The charts which had been dominated by American artists at the beginning of the decade were now nearly the sole preserve of British acts. Only Roy Orbison and The Supremes had a number one single in the UK in 1964. Amongst the British number ones were singles by the Dave Clark Five, The Searchers, The Animals and the Kinks. To show the wide range of popular artists now visiting Manchester, the iconic soul singer Dusty Springfield and Bobby Vee were at the Opera House in May 1964, whilst just outside the city centre, the BBC's Dickenson Road studies in Rusholme had a regular, very significant show for popular music called 'Top of the Pops'. There was no doubt that younger people were throwing off the restrictions they had felt they had been born into. As was seen by the disturbances in Brighton in May 1964 when the Mods and Rockers had clashed, younger people were now concerned about how they looked, how they dressed, both boys & girls. Hairstyles for instance popularised by The Beatles and Rolling Stones in music and quickly carried on by the young Manchester United footballer George Best, saw young men having longer hair than had been seen during the years of National Service, indeed, males seemed to be liking longer hair and females shorter styles perpetuated by such as Twiggy later in the 1960s.

Manchester's own Herman and the Hermits topped the charts with "I'm Into Something Good". A song that was resurrected recently by United fans while under the management of Jose Mourinho. If the sentiment proved to be ill-founded under Mourinho, as we will see, in the summer of 1964 United fans were right to believe that they were indeed into something good…

Saturday 22 August 1964 heralded a transformation in the way football was viewed on television, the start of 'Match of the Day' on BBC TV, via their relatively new channel BBC2. The game televised later that night was Liverpool v Arsenal at Anfield, as Liverpool were the champions. Famously the highlight showed the Kop singing along to 'the Beatles' 'She Loves You'. The same day, over in Manchester, United hosted West Bromwich Albion. The programme featured an artist's impression of how the new cantilever stand would look; the stand included the innovation of private boxes which would come to represent the beginnings of a change in the way people would view matches.

A 2-2 draw against West Bromwich Albion was a slow start for a side now having such an exciting forward line. More disappointments would come in an away defeat at West Ham United and a draw at Leicester City. Although the West Ham result was avenged when the Londoners visited Old Trafford when Fulham won at Craven Cottage alarm bells began to ring. This game would be the first that featured Manchester United on 'Match of the Day'. Fair to say it would not be the last over the years!

Matt Busby was in no mood to hang around. For the next match, away at Everton, he made the subtle change of bringing in a new inexperienced goalkeeper Irishman Pat Dunne who had signed from Shamrock Rovers in the summer, for David Gaskell and restoring David Herd to centre-forward after a rare loss of form. The game signalled a change in this Manchester United side and, arguably, turned them into one of the club's finest. By the end of the season, they would be champions for the first time since the Munich Air Disaster, semi-finalists in the FA Cup (losing in a replay) and semi-finalists in the Inter-Cities Fairs Cup (now Europa League) beaten in a playoff match away in Budapest. They would do this all effectively with only 11 players playing for virtually all the remaining matches, indeed ten of them played 55 or more of the 60 fixtures played in the three competitions, and it would have been 11 if Denis Law had not been sent off again limiting him to 52 of the 60 matches played.

Those 11 who all played at Goodison Park in what was a thrilling 3-3 draw were, Pat Dunne, Brennan, Tony Dunne, Crerand, Foulkes, Stiles, Connelly, Charlton, Herd, Law and Best. Manchester United would go onto play another 18 matches before suffering a defeat.

As if to confirm that like society, football was also changing forever, George Best would make his indelible mark this season, both on and off the pitch. His displays on either wing were sensational for a young man of 18. He stood out for the team despite having two of the all-time greats of the game, Bobby Charlton and Denis Law alongside him. His every move was examined under the microscope that came with being a Manchester United footballer. Off the field he also began to attract the attention of the press. The interest he generated went far beyond the football pages, though. Wherever United played huge crowds swelled attendances to see the young magician play. On 30 September 1964, he travelled with the Manchester United team to play the then league leaders, Chelsea, in London. A crowd of 60,789 flocked to Stamford Bridge to see Best play, witnessing a marvellous display by George as he and Denis Law scored the goals that won the match 2-0. In comparison, a fortnight earlier the attendance was some 38,000 to see Chelsea play Leeds United. Beyond the sensational arrival of Best, the result showed the football world that Manchester United were now well and truly on their way back to the heights of the mid-1950s.

What made this match so symbolic, was that Chelsea's ground, Stamford Bridge, lay just off the Kings Road. The Kings Road had gained itself a reputation as the centre of sixties society. Young mods would meet in its many bars and eating places and visit the clothes shops which by now had been renamed 'boutiques'. Later that year the fashion designer Mary Quant named one of her dress styles the Mini in respect to the fashionable car which had become the car to be seen with. Times they were a-changing, people were dressing for themselves, following fashion became more than cool, it became essential. George Best was the embodiment of this revolution.

The 2-0 defeat of the then league leaders Chelsea put United only two points behind them. On the Saturday following the Chelsea midweek match, George was playing for Northern Ireland against England at Windsor Park Belfast in front of a crowd over 58,000 with Bobby Charlton playing opposite him. Now, in what seems incredible in today's world, Manchester United were playing at Burnley in the league the same day, drawing 0-0. In those days, internationals took precedence, and you just had to get on and field reserve players.

Manchester United's reserves were in great hands then mind you, with Wilf McGuinness taking the reins as the coach. Wilf had a fine footballing career cruelly stopped when he broke his leg in late 1959, ironically in a reserve match when he had been dropped after a dip in form which had seen him capped for England. A man who truly loves Manchester United, Wilf McGuinness is brilliant company and will feature a lot more as we go through the 1960s. He would lead the United reserve side to the top of the league for most of the season before finally finishing in third position.

Besides challenging for the First Division title, United were competing for the first time in the Inter-Cities Fairs Cup, which in 2019 is titled the Europa League. Their first opponents over two legs were the Swedish side Djurgardens. The away leg was first, and United had to make a change from their settled side as Denis Law, after scoring 11 goals in the first 12 league matches, had an injury, so Maurice Setters earned a recall. The tie ended in a 1-1 draw with David Herd scoring the United goal. He would have a memorable league match against Aston Villa at Old Trafford before the 2nd leg was played. David was one of Manchester United's great centre-forwards. A prolific scorer, he was undervalued during his time at Old Trafford playing in the shadows of Law, Best and Charlton, but when you look back at his record, he was a vital player. He explained to Roy Cavanagh in an interview about what he considered his finest ever Manchester United appearance in the Villa match.

'I suppose it is a surprise to many people, considering I scored a couple of goals in an FA Cup Final and also represented my country, that my favourite match was an ordinary league game against Aston Villa in October 1964. We had been playing very well, but I remember Bobby Charlton dropping out just before the kick-off and I wondered if this would affect us. Villa started better than us and should have scored

really before John Connelly produced a brilliant cross for a centre-forward, but I honestly felt it was the best headed goal of my career, it fairly flew home! Denis Law then scored a couple of long-range efforts, which Bobby would have been proud of, and then a couple in his own style to claim four goals for himself, Connelly got one and I scored another to leave us 7-0 winners. This proved to us all I think that we were a very good side because Bobby had been playing some of his finest ever football and we had won 7-0 without him.'

Interestingly, the crowd for the Aston Villa match was only 35,809, part of an overall season average of 44,886 with the lowest being for a rearranged midweek match against Birmingham City of 25,721. While football was still a very popular sport and money for pastimes was not flowing for the working masses now, particularly the young were finding other ways of wanting to spend their money on themselves.

When United then put six past Djurgardens in the 2nd leg at Old Trafford and then went to Liverpool and beat the champions 2-0 on their own pitch to go top of the table, the feeling that we were watching something special just grew.

Dortmund Borussia from Germany had been Manchester United's second opponent in the European Cup back in 1956. The two-legged tie had seen the home leg for United played at Maine Road as Old Trafford would not have their lights switched on until the following March. A 3-2 home victory was completed with a battling 0-0 draw in Germany to put United in the quarter-finals. In November 1964 the roles were reversed with the first match in Germany, only for Manchester United to produce one of their greatest ever results, winning 6-1 away from home! The 2nd leg was always going to be a formality after that, but still United overpowered Dortmund 4-0 to go through 10-1 on aggregate against a top-class side who were second in the German league at the time.

Just when it seemed nothing could stop Manchester United, for the second season running, Denis Law was sent off earning him a lengthy suspension. Denis was involved in an incident with the young Blackpool player Alan Ball and saw red. It did not stop United winning though, and their 2-1 victory kept them top of the table. Before the suspension took effect, United's position was further consolidated with victories over Blackburn at home and Arsenal away, before the resurgent Leeds United, promoted back to the First Division for the first time in four years visited Old Trafford.

Manchester United were three points clear of Chelsea and four ahead of Leeds when the Yorkshire side arrived at Old Trafford. Starting with the 3-3 draw at Everton back in September, Manchester United had played 19 matches unbeaten in the league and the Inter-Cities Fairs Cup, but all good things come to an end, and it was Leeds, with Johnny Giles in their side, who went home with the points after a 1-0 victory. Leeds had gone out of their way to stop George Best; their very experienced inside forward Bobby Collins had kicked him viciously as the game neared half-time, which prompted Nobby Stiles to take Collins out every time he came near him. This Leeds match marked the beginning of a rivalry which has become very intense between the United's of Manchester and Leeds. There was, of course, a starting point of the traditional cross Pennines rivalry between clubs from Lancashire and Yorkshire, but this match would symbolise a battle for ideas too. A battle between expansive, attacking football and a more pragmatic, defensive approach. Beyond even this, there was a typically dramatic incident in this match, that the well-respected referee, the late Jim Finney from Hereford, explained to Roy Cavanagh.

'The match was very tense, Manchester well on top in the first-half, with Gary Sprake making at least three tremendous saves, one form Bobby Charlton and two from Denis Law. George Best took a knock late on in the half which made him a virtual passenger, and with Leeds having eight or nine back in defence they looked well happy with a draw. However, Bobby Collins nicked one in a breakaway, and it looked like they would take both points back to Yorkshire. During most of the match, a typical Manchester mist had rung around, but to make matters worse with about 15 minutes left, a steam train pulled into the nearby railway station and bellowed its smoke over the ground. I simply could not see, in fact when two players went past me and I did not know who they were, I said, that's it, I will have to take the teams off before somebody gets hurt. With both sides back in their dressing rooms, Don Revie, nearly begging on his hands and knees, came up to me, the veins sticking out in his neck shouting that Leeds were 1-0 up and I couldn't possibly abandon the match. In contrast, Matt Busby calmly asked to be kept informed. After about ten minutes or so, I decided to go and take a look in the middle, when as I got to the pitch edge, a massive copper grabbed hold of me and said, 'nobody goes on that pitch' Quite right I said, taking off my overcoat to reveal my referees top, not until I let them! Eventually, the game continued, and Leeds held out for their victory.'

The suspension for Denis Law that began after the Leeds match was for a month as opposed to a fixed number of matches played. In a way, bad weather helped United as a couple of games were called off around Christmas 1964, but it seemed an unsatisfactory way of dealing with matters. Law frequently seemed to have issues with referees around Christmas time. There had been the controversy with the referee in the West Bromwich Albion game of 1962, the sending off at Aston Villa in 1963 and now the sending off at Blackpool in 1964. Perhaps there was a vendetta by the referees against Denis before the festive period? At the time, there were some United supporter's that believed Denis wanted a suspension to go home to Scotland for Christmas and the New Year - you paid your money and took your choice!

By the time Denis returned, for the away match at Nottingham Forest on the 16 January 1965, Manchester United had drawn three and won just one in the league. They had also overcome Fourth Division Chester in the 3rd round FA Cup tie, where another member of the successful FA Youth Cup team the previous season, Albert Kinsey had a goal-scoring debut in United's 2-1 victory.

Manchester United, with Denis Law back, and scoring two goals at Forest in a 2-2 draw, now had a daunting fixture list in front of them with participation in two cup competitions while simultaneously leading the race for the First Division title. The Inter-Cities Fairs Cup provided, for the second season running, a European fixture with an English side - this time Everton. As expected, the two ties were very tight affairs with John Connelly showing his worth yet again by scoring United's goal in a 1-1 Old Trafford draw and scoring and then creating the winner for David Herd over at Goodison Park as United won through 3-2 on aggregate.

From one cup to another, this time the FA Cup which drew United away at Stoke City. In what would become a common theme in the following FA Cup ties, United would play their opponents in round 4, 5 and 6 in the league the week before the cup tie. Stoke City were first up, with a team that included two former Manchester United captains in Dennis Viollet and Maurice Setters. The latter had moved only the previous November after four seasons at Old Trafford. Maurice had won the cup with United in 1963, but the performances of Nobby Stiles in the number six shirt had convinced Matt Busby that Nobby was one for now, and the future. A great choice by Matt as it turned out!

Although closely marked by Setters, Denis Law scored United's goal in a 1-1 draw before the sides met at the Victoria Ground in Stoke for the 4th round of the FA Cup. There had been a real expectation that Stanley Matthews would make what was now becoming a rare appearance for Stoke in this match but, eventually, an injury ruled him out just days before his 50th birthday. Stanley Matthews had been firmly in the news since the New Year's Honours list when the relatively new Prime Minister Harold Wilson had flexed his muscles with his civil servants. Wilson realised the popularity of football and quickly moved to turn it to his advantage by recommending Stanley Matthews, already a CBE, for what would be the first professional Knighthood. The award of such an honour to a sportsman went against tradition and was challenged by the authorities prompting Harold Wilson to ask the question, *'Who has the final decision?'*, *'You do'* was the answer, *'In that case he receives it'* was the final decision of the Huddersfield Town supporting Prime Minister!

It was another former Prime Minister who made the news on Saturday 30 January 1965, as Sir Winston Churchill, the man who had courageously led Britain's fight for freedom against the Germans in the Second World War, was laid to rest in a state funeral, the first of a non-royal Family member since 1935. There have been none since. While the whole country was in mourning with the event televised live to the nation, the 4th round FA Cup tie at Stoke finished in a 0-0 draw, United's sixth draw in eight matches, meaning that a third meeting in 11 days was needed between the clubs. At Old Trafford, a threatening mist once again made viewing late on in the match very difficult, but it held off enough for a David Herd goal to win the match for United and a prize of a home tie against Burnley in the next round.

The Seventh anniversary of the Munich Air Disaster on Saturday 6 February 1965 saw Manchester United playing at Tottenham Hotspur. United v Spurs is always one of the most eagerly anticipated fixtures of the year. Both sides have a reputation to this day of playing entertaining football. The game was changing though as more defensive sides were coming to the fore. No doubt Matt Busby possibly still had Leeds United in mind when he said the following in the Daily Mirror on the morning of the game in an article titled 'I Promise You a Game to Remember':

I PROMISE YOU A GAME TO REMEMBER—BUSBY

'We want to beat Spurs, but I promise you that I would rather lose than get involved in what is going on in football at the moment. I hate defensive football, I want no part in it, and I can promise you that so long as I have anything to do with it, Manchester United will never play it. The very thought of playing against Spurs is like a breath of fresh air after what we have faced in recent matches, overloaded defences, packed penalty areas.'

Many believed at the time that the game had moved on, and the likes of Matt Busby were unable to adapt to a new way of playing football. He would prove his doubters wrong in emphatic style. The result didn't go United's way, but for Roy Cavanagh, there was certainly a most interesting afternoon, if not a game to remember!

'I still recall a most basic error I made at this match. Being a bit flash by taking a young lady I was going out with to Tottenham, and I assumed that the ground must be near the Tottenham Court Road. Doh! By the time I found out there was a distance of about eight miles, it was an urgent call for a taxi! But by the time we crawled near to White Hart Lane the traffic was stopped and the crowds enormous. Out of the taxi to try and get to the ground, we were faced with more people going the other way as news came back gates closed nearly an hour from kick-off! That United lost 1-0 made the day longer, although the lady brightened up as she realised, we were on the same train as the returning Manchester United side and a certain George Best!'

Manchester United show their class

Goals galore at Molineux

By ERIC TODD: Wolverhampton Wnds. 3, Manchester Utd. 5

At least United soon got back to winning ways, firstly defeating Burnley in the league match and repeating the feat in the FA Cup tie, both at Old Trafford. The pattern of meeting a side in the league and then the cup continued with matches against Wolverhampton Wanderers. First a home victory in the league and then a memorable sixth round tie at Molineux. The original tie had to be called off on the Saturday as heavy snow hit Wolverhampton, but a full house of 53,000 turned up on Wednesday evening and was ecstatic as the home side went 2-0 up. This fine Manchester United side, however, was in no mood to let one of their trophy targets slip and came back to win 5-3 in an unforgettable match.

In the mid-sixties, for some reason, Manchester United played a lot of Monday night matches and one of them, against Fulham, quickly followed a vital top of the table league match with Chelsea. The visit of the two London sides produced two excellent victories 4-0 and 4-1 respectively. George Best was now very aware that anything he did against a London club would create twice the news as other matches, so his exquisite lob from close to the by-line over the Chelsea keeper Peter Bonetti is still shown regularly 54 years on whenever the Belfast genius is remembered.

With fixtures piling up, the last thing Manchester United needed was a replay in the FA Cup semi-final against Leeds United, and they also did not need the sheer physical effect of those games either. The first match was played at Hillsborough, home of Sheffield Wednesday and a clogging mud-laden pitch was a factor in spoiling a match where players from both sides spent a lot of the time attacking each other as it ended goalless. Both sides were also fighting for the First Division title, but it would be Leeds United that secured a Wembley appearance in the final against Liverpool with a last-minute Billy Bremner goal in the replay played at Nottingham Forest's City Ground.

Following the earlier situation this season when Manchester United, and others had to play matches despite their players being involved in international matches, a rule was passed saying that if four players from a club were selected, the league match could be postponed. Saturday 10 April 1965 was a case in point, as four United players, Denis Law and Pat Crerand for Scotland and Bobby Charlton and Nobby Stiles for England were called up to play in the England v Scotland match at Wembley Stadium. The match was Nobby's international debut, and he told Roy Cavanagh of an amusing incident that happened in the tunnel before the game. *'I was lining up for my debut, feeling the nerves naturally, when I saw my teammate Denis Law coming alongside in the Scotland line up. I looked across and asked him how he was and got a right mouthful where to go!'* Roy actually went to this match and still remembers the Scottish fans hanging out of cars and taxis *shouting, 'we are the people.'* The international ended 2-2, played in pouring rain with England gearing up for the World Cup the following summer.

Forty-Eight hours later, Nobby, along with Bobby and Pat, were all teammates again as United played once more on a Monday night, this time at home to Leicester City. A 1-0 victory was achieved without Denis Law, injured when Nobby had kicked him in the international! A young lad from the reserves, John Aston, made his Manchester United debut in this match.

Easter 1965 was always going to be a crucial period in determining the destination of the First Division title. Indeed, the league match at Elland Road between Leeds United and Manchester United on Easter Saturday was likely to settle that destination. Leeds, of course, had already won two of the three meetings between the sides 1-0 and as the other had ended 0-0, it meant Manchester had not scored a goal against Leeds this season. They did this time, a goal from John Connelly won the match, probably also repaying his transfer fee as the title was Manchester United's to lose now.

The last weekend in April 1965 gave United the opportunity to win the First Division title at Old Trafford for the first time since 1957 and the following year's Munich Air Disaster. On Saturday the 24th, FA Cup finalists Liverpool visited, while on Monday night Arsenal were the opposition. Liverpool seemed to have their minds on the following Saturday's final at Wembley Stadium against Leeds United, and a marvellous display from United proved far too much for them, with Denis Law scoring another two goals in a 3-0 victory, but he also picked up another knock which certainly caused alarm bells ringing for Matt Busby.

PAGE 26   DAILY MIRROR, Tuesday, April 27, 1965

Manchester United champs..

'CRIPPLED' LAW THE HERO WITH TWO GOALS

Manchester United 3, Arsenal 1

In the end, Matt had Denis patched up with a tight bandage around his knee for the visit of Arsenal, on the same night Leeds United were away at Birmingham City for their last fixture, United still having a rearranged game at Villa Park on Wednesday if they needed. An expectant crowd of over 50,000 were at Old Trafford for yet another Monday night match with the crowd just as concerned with news filtering through from the Midlands from Birmingham's match with Leeds. Certainly, Arsenal were in more of a mood to give United a match than cup finalists Liverpool had been the previous Saturday. Denis Law, however, was irresistible, injured or not, and he was the man who carried Manchester United to their sixth league title. Two goals from him and one from George Best ensured a 3-1 victory which was punctured at times by roars as radios picked up that Leeds were a goal down, then 3-0 down, before the roars turned to nervous 'ooh's' as Leeds threatened a comeback at 3-2. Those scores remained the same, however, and although the teams were level on points, Manchester United had a vastly superior goal difference, scoring more and conceding less than Leeds and unless they lost 19-0 at Villa Park on Wednesday, the title was theirs. The scenes at Old Trafford had to be seen to be believed as the sheer emotion of what Manchester United had been through since their last title in April 1957 unfurled. The ultimate mathematical confirmation was delivered on the Wednesday at Villa Park when a still celebrating United lost 2-1.

Denis Law scored 28 goals in 36 league matches, with his fellow forwards, John Connelly, Bobby Charlton, David Herd and George Best all scoring double figures. The half-back line of Pat Crerand, Bill Foulkes and Nobby Stiles provided flair, steel and experience, whilst behind them completing a team of internationals, the three Irishmen, goalkeeper Pat Dunne, Shay Brennan and Tony Dunne all played their roles perfectly, in Tony Dunne's case to the highest level, he was a real top-class full-back. Tony Dunne, Brennan, Foulkes and Connelly each played in all 60 competitive matches that season with Charlton, Best and Stiles missing just one with 59 appearances. As you would expect the average crowds were up again at Old Trafford this time to 45,831. Football crowds generally were down though, but the visit of Manchester United put thousands on away crowds, with fans desperate to the see the sensation that was George Best. United's matches in London, in particular, attracted huge crowds. We've already mentioned the crowd of 60,769 at Chelsea compared to an average gate of just over 37,000. The attendances of 59,627 at Arsenal; 58,639 at Spurs; 37,070 at West Ham and 36,291 at Fulham compared to average crowds of just 31,327 (Arsenal); 39,391 (Spurs); 25,858 (West Ham) and 17,563 at Fulham. There are many reasons that Manchester United have a large support in London, but the glamour that United brought to the capital in those mid-sixties games is surely a big factor.

Pos	Club	Pld	W	D	L	GF	GA	Pts
1	Manchester United	42	26	9	7	89	39	61
2	Leeds United	42	26	9	7	83	52	61
3	Chelsea	42	24	8	10	89	54	56

Manchester United were most definitely back, but they still had an opportunity to win the club's first-ever European trophy, the Inter-Cities Fairs Cup. As was still the way of arranging matches in Europe in 1965, the dates were to be arranged by the competing clubs and, incredibly, the quarter-final ties between United and Racing Club of Strasbourg were not played until the league was well and truly completed on the 12th and 19th May. Away in France, against a side that had knocked out both Barcelona and AC Milan, Manchester United went and won 5-0. The second-leg at Old Trafford was a non-event but was preceded by a well-deserved presentation to Denis Law, that of European Footballer of the Year. Even Denis was not in a scoring mood after such an emotional honour and his side already being 5-0 up, with a 0- 0 draw ensuing.

Over a month after lifting the League title, Manchester United were still playing football, and at the highest level of a European competition semi-final. So, well before Monday night being a thing for Sky TV, Monday 31 May 1965 saw a visit from the Hungarian side Ferencvaros. Their star player was centre-forward Florian Albert, joint top scorer at the 1962 World Cup finals, but he would not be on the score sheet for a tie which extended to three matches and was only completed on 16 June!

Old Trafford saw a niggly match which United came from a goal down to lead comfortably 3-1 late on, only fatefully to take their foot off the pedal. A late second goal for the Hungarians would prove vital. The second leg in Budapest ended in a 1-0 victory for the home side, where the niggle carried over from the first leg with Pat Crerand, and a Hungarian sent off. The match was tied on aggregate, resulting in a toss-up for venue of the third match. Ferencvaros won that, and a now tired Manchester United could not raise themselves yet again and lost 2-1. Such was the lateness of these matches that the final was arranged over a single tie, Juventus won the toss to stage it but, incredibly, Ferencvaros went to Turin and won the Fairs Cup 1-0.

A shorter summer break set the platform for what would be a momentous following season for football, the World Cup finals being staged in England and Manchester United competing in the European Cup again…

.

Chapter Seven

EL BEATLE!

1965-66

The summer of 1965 was marked by the sad news that, at the age of 83, Manchester United's chairman, Harold Hardman, had passed away, on 9 June 1965. Harold Hardman is one of a number of largely unsung heroes in the history of the club. He was a remarkable character – whose association with the club he loved started in 1908 and finished that summer some 57 years later. Born in Manchester in 1882 he was a frail boy, his doctor saying that he 'was not strong enough to play games'. His parents moved to Blackpool where they hoped the sea air would be better for the young Harold's health. Despite his doctor's advice, Harold took up football with notable success using his physique to his advantage as an elusive and speedy outside-left. He made his debut for Blackpool FC aged 18 and stayed there for three years, before moving to Everton for five years, playing in the FA Cup Finals in 1906 and 1907. Outside football he enjoyed success too. Appointed as a solicitor in Manchester in 1907 he played four games at United in 1908 before moving on to Bradford City and Stoke finishing his playing career in 1913. During his career he played four times for England and was a gold medallist with the Great Britain Football Team in the 1908 Olympics. He remains the only English Gold Medallist to have played for United. In 1912 he was appointed as a director at Manchester United. Apart from the one brief period during troubled times in the early 1930s, he remained a director for the rest of his life. He became chairman of the club in 1951 after the death of James W. Gibson. During his time as chairman he oversaw United's three league title glories of the 1950s as well as their early adventures in the European Cup from 1956 to 1958. His greatest challenge at the club was to provide a steady hand at the time of the Munich air disaster on 6 February 1958. Although he would not have dared imagine it at the time, the success United enjoyed in the 60s provides testament to his leadership which is epitomised by the famous article 'United Will Go On' that he wrote for the match programme for United's first game after Munich against Sheffield Wednesday. We reproduce that article below.

'It is the sad duty of we who serve United to offer the bereaved our heartfelt sympathy and condolences. Here is a tragedy which will sadden us for years to come, but in this we are not alone. An unprecedented blow to British football has touched the hearts of millions and we express our deep gratitude to the many who have sent messages of sympathy and floral tributes.

Wherever football is played United is mourned, but we rejoice that so many of our party have been spared and we wish them a speedy and complete recovery.

 Words are inadequate to describe our thanks and appreciation to the truly magnificent work of the surgeons and nurses of the Rechts der Isar Hospital at Munich. But for their superb skill and deep compassion our casualties must have been greater. To Professor Georg Maurer, Chief Surgeon, we offer our eternal gratitude.

 Although we mourn our dead and grieve for our wounded we believe that great days are not done for us. The sympathy and encouragement of the football world and particularly our supporters will justify and inspire us.

 The road back may be long and hard but the memory of those who died at Munich, of their stirring achievements and wonderful sportsmanship ever with us, Manchester United will rise again.'

H.P. Hardman. Chairman.

Rise again United did, and it must have given Harold Hardman huge pleasure to see Manchester United win the league for the first time since Munich in May 1965. United, then known as Newton Heath, were only four-years-old when he was born, and the change of chairmanship from Hardman to Louis Edwards marked a turning point in United's history.

Now half-way through the decade, life was changing for society too, as expectations continued to rise all around. Living conditions, finally, began to improve as the slums were being finally eradicated. Manchester and Salford for example, relocated thousands of people to areas away from the city centres, Salford people going away to live in Little Hulton close to Bolton and Irlam on the way to Warrington, Manchester folk to areas like Wythenshawe – Europe's biggest ever council estate. These new houses included basic needs such as indoor toilets and a proper bathroom with central heating provided. People, at last, felt as though they had something to build on, particularly the younger ones seeing a hopeful future.

The football experience was also changing, as one looking around Old Trafford could see as the building of the new cantilever stand was underway. So far in the 60s, a match day would be a male-dominated experience, thousands of men in flat caps, cigarettes very likely being smoked. When capacity crowds filled a stadium, the crush made for unpleasant situations, no time or space to say *'excuse me while I go to the toilet'* you just had to make your own arrangement such was the crush! Unless a very important cup tie, it would normally be 'pay at the gate', with standing accounting for the vast majority of space, Old Trafford until the cantilever opened, having only two or three thousand seats in a 65,000 capacity.

If not a full house, the opportunity to change ends at half-time was a plus. After the game, the likelihood was that you would be walking home or catching a bus, or for those going into Manchester travelling by the special trains that ran alongside the main stand area. Pre-match and half-time entertainment until the mid-1960s was provided by the Beswick Prize Band

and their vocalist Sylvia Farmer, they incidentally also provided this at Maine Road when United were away. By the mid-1960s, facilities were starting to improve, certainly when the cantilever opened with facilities only imagined in the wildest dreams of the majority of supporters.

Manchester itself provided many different forms of entertainment, from the Belle Vue complex where stars of the music world would appear alongside the many top bouts of boxing and regular wrestling contests. A fine speedway team and greyhound racing made it a place to take oneself away from life's mundane times. In the city centre, the new music and dancing scene brought youngsters into it with places like the Plaza and the Ritz very popular, while drinking places called Bier Kellers also being enjoyed as the 60s generation felt they had a life to live to the full now.

For the more sophisticated, two or three drinking and eating places to be seen included the Cromford Club near where the Arndale Centre is now, the Sportsman's Club on Market Street or the Cabaret Club opposite the Odeon Cinema on Oxford Road. In his book 'Best and Edwards' Gordon Burn describes how Matt Busby enjoyed his part in Manchester nightlife *'[He] was no playboy, but he loved characters whose spirits were freer than his own. He loved Manchester, its looseness, its joie de vivre, its tolerance. Matt didn't play, but he liked to spectate. To be in the company of larger-than-life characters in his leisure time.'* It was the Cromford Club that became the haunt of Matt Busby and Jean his wife, often joined by Louis Edwards and his wife and such as Johnny Foy one of Manchester's top bookmakers. Owned by a former boxer Paddy McGrath, it was him who encouraged and supported Matt Busby to fight on at United, providing money to sign Ernie Taylor from Blackpool for example in the darkest hour after Munich. It was the 'in' place for people who wanted to be seen mingling with the stars of stage screen and sport. Jackie Blanchflower who suffered so badly in the crash was supported by his wife Jean who was a very classy singer at the Cromford Club, and her encouragement helped Jackie move into activities such as after-dinner speaking where he was very good and funny. In later times, Paddy McGrath sold the Cromford Club to Hugh Heffner for another one of his Playboy Clubs.

As champions, Manchester United welcomed cup holders Liverpool to Old Trafford in August 1965 for the Charity Shield, with the magnificent new cantilever stand completed and a new world of football watching dawning. It was also the first official football match in England with substitutes, with Willie Anderson the honour of being Manchester United's, although, with respect to Willie, who replaced the injured Denis Law early in the match, it was not a swop that had been envisaged by Matt Busby. Substitutions were only permitted for an injured player for the next two seasons before they were allowed for tactical reasons as well. A fine match ended 2-2, in those days there was no extra-time or penalties, so the shield was shared by each side for six months apiece.

A very sluggish start by United included a 4-2 defeat at Nottingham Forest, then managed by Johnny Carey one of the greatest ever footballers to play for Manchester United and Ireland. Ten points from ten matches was not the start of champions. Away from the League though the first European Cup tie at Old Trafford since the ill-fated 1958 season brought the champions of Finland, H.J.K Helsinki who were summarily sent home with a 6-0 defeat which following United's 3-2 victory in Helsinki gave United a comfortable passage into the last 16.

During October 1965 Matt Busby celebrated 20 years as the manager of Manchester United. His success in that role was mightily impressive at that time. Four League Championships, six times runners-up, two FA Cup triumphs, two losing finals and a further eight losses at the semi-final stage, six times winners of the FA Youth Cup and two semi semi-finals in the European Cup, a competition which had also seen one of football's greatest ever sides wiped out. Only Ernest Magnall had led United to League and FA Cup triumphs before, elsewhere only Herbert Chapman when at Huddersfield Town and Arsenal had a record that could compare to Busby's, although European and FA Youth cup competition was not in place during Chapman's successful seasons.

On the pitch, the anniversary was hardly celebrated in the style it deserved. The Manchester United players presented Matt Busby with a handmade cut glass vase before the match at Tottenham Hotspur which was closest to his anniversary. They chose the occasion to be outplayed by a marvellous Spurs display that lit up the Match of the Day programme later that Saturday evening by winning 5-1. The match included a quite wonderful goal by Jimmy Greaves, described by Matt Busby himself as 'one of the best goals I've seen in 20 years' and still shown whenever matches between these two great clubs are recalled.

This crushing defeat woke Manchester United up as they ended their mediocre start by going on a 12-match unbeaten run, including further progress in the European Cup as they beat A.S.K. Vorwarts, of, the still then, East Germany, 6-0 over the two legs. One of the biggest problems in facing Eastern European sides in the 1960s was the issue of visas and although Manchester United had done their best to ease the process, getting through the Berlin wall crossing caused an issue. Allegedly, Pat Crerand said his name was James Bond, causing a delay of over three hours which did not endear Pat to his teammates or Matt Busby!

Amongst the victories in the league during this unbeaten run was the return fixture with Tottenham Hotspur, again a Match of the Day featured match, with an exact reversal of the previous match in October as United won 5-1. Although there was a lot of rain about, this match only drew a crowd of 39,511, which highlighted a large drop generally in attendances around the country, despite the imminent arrival of the World Cup Finals in England in the summer of 1966. Manchester United had been affected by these drops in crowds, the league average at the end of the season would be 41,352 with crowds varying from a high of 58,161 v Liverpool to a low of just 23,039 at the season's end against Aston Villa. The two European Cup matches so far had both only attracted 30,000, but that competition and the FA Cup would attract full house gates for the games to come.

Having had a very settled side the previous season, this season saw injuries cause changes with the goalkeeping position seeing Pat Dunne, David Gaskell and Harry Gregg each making their mark. Harry Gregg is a marvellous man, a hero in fact on and off the pitch. His actions in a blazing aeroplane on the runway at Munich airport in February 1958 will never be forgotten by Manchester United followers. His goalkeeping ability also earned the tag fearless, many a time to Harry's disadvantage as he suffered far too many injuries in his Old Trafford career, depriving him of appearances in a 1963 FA Cup Final victory and enough league appearance for a 1965 league winners medal. Cruelly, for such a great servant who made a total of 247 appearances for the club, ill-timed injuries would mean he would end his career at United without a winners medal to his name.

Another Manchester United great, Denis Law suffered an injury in the drawn league match against West Ham United which would have serious repercussions for his native Scotland. With England automatically qualified as hosts for the 1966 World Cup Finals, many people felt Scotland would also have their finest chance of success if they qualified. To do so they needed to beat Italy away, but Law's injury meant he missed the match and the Italians won comfortably 3-0 to qualify.

The next generation of Manchester United players appeared as the FA Youth Cup commenced with a resounding 5-0 victory over local rivals City with United's new star being a local Manchester lad called Brian Kidd. Sadly, they got knocked out at Liverpool in the next round but team members Brian, and also a Scottish lad called Francis Burns, would play in a

European champions squad a few years later...

Manchester United's unbeaten run of 12 matches came to an end in a marvellous top of the table match away at Liverpool on New Year's Day 1966 when they lost 2-1 to the side that would eventually win the title. The defeat preceded the start of the FA Cup and the quarter-finals of the European Cup against the magnificent Portuguese champions Benfica. In the previous five seasons, Benfica had been winners twice and runners-up twice in that competition. Far from being deflated by the Liverpool defeat, United went on another long unbeaten run, this time of 13 games as they progressed into the later stages of both cups and maintained a challenge in the league.

The FA Cup draws were kind, pitting Manchester United against Second Division opposition all the way to the semi-final, with ties against Derby County, Rotherham United, Wolverhampton Wanderers and Preston North End. Draws in two of them, against Rotherham and Preston, did not help with the fixture congestion which would occur. Those two matches were played at Old Trafford, with bumper crowds of 54,000 and 60,000 respectively dwarfing the usual crowds at league fixtures.

Those FA Cup attendances were going to be exceeded though as the European Cup came around. For the visit of Benfica in the first leg quarter-final, over 64,000 crammed into Old Trafford. United, played in all white as it was the home side which changed shirts in this competition. A United side full of international players, ten of them vastly experienced along with the youthfulness of their young prodigy George Best, were in perfect form to take on their excellent opposition. A tremendous end to end match saw Benfica score first before David Herd, and Denis Law made it 2-1 to United at half-time. The Benfica defence were approaching the later stage of their marvellous careers, and United's speed of attack was wearing them down. A third goal from the most unlikely source of centre-half Bill Foulkes, one of three Munich survivors playing for United in this match (Harry Gregg and Bobby Charlton the other two) put United 3-1 up midway through the second half with a real chance of qualifying. When Benfica's giant centre-forward Torres scored from a defensive mistake to reduce the deficit to 3-2, the advantage had swung the way of the visitors.

Manchester United though had one of their greatest ever forward lines, Showing the total flexibility of the five players, from the previous season they had all changed position with wingers Connelly and Best switching from numbers 11 and 7, Charlton going from number 8 to 9, Herd from 9 to 10 and Law from 10 to 8. Five marvellous footballers and all with goals in them. For one of them, George Best, the return in Lisbon was going to transform him from a footballer to an international icon...

As we saw in the previous chapter, George Best had already made headlines in England, helping United to draw huge crowds wherever they played. For George though, the 9th March in the beautiful city of Lisbon saw him explode onto the world scene as he destroyed one of Europe's greatest sides Benfica 5-1 on their own pitch! That night George Best became the Beatles, Rolling Stones, Twiggy, the King's Road and David Bailey all into one. He was 19 years old and was instantly the front and back pages of the still powerful newspapers of the time. So much so, that when he got back to his digs at Mrs Fullaway's, there were 5,000 letters waiting for him!

The evening got off to an interesting start with Pat Crerand smashing a mirror in the dressing rooms in a kick about to incur the wrath of Matt Busby who knew all about the supposed seven years bad luck such a thing was imagined to bring. No need to worry though, as what followed is one of the finest displays by a Manchester United side, described by Matt Busby as 'our finest hour'. David Herd, one of the Manchester United forwards that night, recalled the game in an interview to Roy Cavanagh.

'Benfica tried to put us off before the kick-off, which was already going to be 9 pm. We must have been kicking in for about ten minutes (remember those were the days when teams just came out before the kick-off, no pitch preparations of half-hour or so like today) when Eusebio appeared to receive his European Footballer of the Year award, with firecrackers going off all around the stadium. Then we got to grips with them and set firecrackers off of our own! Although I did not get on the score sheet, I did get, literally, a hole kicked out of my leg by their big centre half Germano. We were fantastic that night. I felt fortunate to be alongside three world-beaters of our own in Denis, Bobby and George. Denis, sharp as a needle, deadly near goal, Bobby had such a free-flowing style, fantastic body swerve, always unselfish, whilst George had bits of both, a tremendous individual.'

The Lisbon crowd of 75,000 sat back, expecting to watch their side progress to yet another semi-final. George Best though had very different ideas, and inside the first 13 minutes, he had scored twice and had a goal disallowed! A third United goal did come after 20 minutes, and again Best nearly got it before Connelly managed the last touch. 3-0 at half time, 6-2 up on aggregate and even though away goals still did not count, Manchester United were already a large way onto their third semi-final of the European Cup. Indeed, it was Benfica who scored next as Shay Brennan scored an own goal, but inside the last 15 minutes further goals from Crerand and Charlton completed the rout at 5-1, and went a long way to erasing the memory of United's ill-fated visit to the same city two years earlier when Sporting Lisbon had inflicted their record European defeat.

Photographs of George Best, wearing a large sombrero as he arrived back with the team was the start of the press interest in the young 19-year-old Northern Irishman. He was, seriously, now in a different world. It reflected the change in society though; colour was now all around, personalities filled the news both of music, fashion and football with the likes of George all over the papers, magazines as everybody seemed to want to know about him, what he was eating, drinking, wearing. He was a superstar.

On 31 March 1966 Harold Wilson led the Labour Government to another victory in the polls, only this time with a majority of 96 seats, he would remain Prime Minister through the rest of this book's progress in the 1960s.

As April 1966 arrived, Manchester United again faced chronic fixture congestion. They were faced with playing nine matches in 24 days, at a time before the squad system was used, there would be no rotation of players. These games included two European Cup semi-final ties with Partizan Belgrade and an FA Cup semi-final with Everton to be played at Burnden Park home of Bolton Wanderers. We often hear about how the players of today are pampered and that players of the past happily played on week in week out, day in day out. The reality was though that footballers were never supermen, and something had to give. The last days of March finally brought injury disaster to Manchester United. In the away FA Cup tie with Preston North End George Best suffered a bad knee injury which would eventually need a cartilage operation.

Date	Fixture	Competition
Wednesday 6 April	Aston Villa v Manchester United	League Division One
Saturday 9 April	Manchester United v Leicester City	League Division One
Wednesday 13 April	Partizan Belgrade v Manchester United	European Cup
Saturday 16 April	Sheffield United v Manchester United	League Division One
Wednesday 20 April	Manchester United v Partizan Belgrade	European Cup
Saturday 23 April	Everton v Manchester United	FA Cup
Monday 25 April	Everton v Manchester United	League Division One
Wednesday 27 April	Manchester United v Blackpool	League Division One
Saturday 30 April	West Ham United v Manchester United	League Division One

Best tried to play on and gauge how bad the injury was by playing in the league match at home to Leicester City the Saturday before Manchester United would make an emotional journey to Belgrade to play their first leg European Cup semi-final with Partizan. If there was a positive side to the surprise 2-1 home defeat to Leicester, it did at least show the youth production lines at Old Trafford were still working as youngsters Willie Anderson, David Sadler, and a debutant left-back, Bobby Noble were all in the United side alongside the struggling Best. When you added the likes of John Aston, who would play 20 times in all competitions this season, it looked a promising future.

For Harry Gregg, Bill Foulkes, Bobby Charlton and of course, Matt Busby a visit to Belgrade to play a top European match must have had so many emotions, eight years after virtually a full team had been wiped out on the route back from Belgrade. Poignantly, the match was played at the same stadium as Manchester United had played Red Star Belgrade in 1958, as back then the Red Star ground was too small for such a vital match, and the game was transferred to Partizan's ground. After United's great victory over Benfica, they were a feared side, and Partizan certainly started the game on the back foot. Sadly, George Best was not fit and limped off in the second-half, not playing again this season. The home side realised this might be their best chance and secured a two-goal advantage.

The second leg was played the following week with Willie Anderson having the impossible task of replacing George Best. Partizan, aided by a two-goal advantage, were in the mood to defend it - by whatever means necessary. A match that turned into a very physical encounter saw Pat Crerand and a Partizan player sent off, and despite a late goal from Nobby

Stiles, United went out 2-1 on aggregate. What the feeling must have been for Matt Busby is hard to imagine. In two seasons during the 1950s his handpicked side, brim-full of young players nurtured through his youth scheme had reached the semi-final stage and while they failed to progress it seemed only a matter of time before they would develop into European champions. Now in 1966, he had a side that appeared to be the finished article, containing in Bobby Charlton, Denis Law and George Best three of the greatest footballers of all time - but had lost out again. Would Matt want to continue, could the players lift themselves to achieve the dream of everybody connected to Manchester United?

There was still a lot to play for though, and the immediate thought had to be the FA Cup semi-final the coming Saturday against Everton at Bolton. Willie Anderson again was on United's right-wing and looking back it is uncanny how so alike he looked to George Best, similar hairstyle similar style of play but nobody had the gold dust George possessed. A cagey match was settled late on with a goal by a young Colin Harvey for Everton, within the space of 72 hours Manchester United's season had crashed all around them.

While the results in April confirmed a season that promised everything would end in disappointment, the end of April 1966 produced a fitting tribute to Bobby Charlton - the award of Footballer of the Year, the 19th recipient with only Johnny Carey back in 1949 being a fellow Manchester United player. Roy Cavanagh saw the whole of Bobby's career and remembers his impact on the club and the game of football;

'I first saw Bobby Charlton playing for Manchester United's youth team as they marched on regularly winning the youth cup. I also went to more reserve matches in those mid-50s and Bobby was generally played as a centre forward or inside left. What always struck me was that he wanted to shoot! Many a time a ball to him 30 yards out was one thought have a shot at goal. The strength of players around him was frightening, the first team had Whelan, Taylor and Viollet as their inside forwards, while such as Johnny Doherty, Colin Webster and even younger than Bobby, Alex Dawson and Mark Pearson were challenging. Bobby's first-team debut came against his namesake, Charlton Athletic at Old Trafford in October 1956. He was in because Tommy Taylor was playing for England, but Bobby scored twice as United won 4-2. For the next 14 months, he was in and out of the side replacing any of the recognised inside-forward trio. By December 1957 Matt Busby decided it was his time and he replaced Billy Whelan permanently. He was in the side the day before the air crash scoring in Belgrade as United drew 3-3. The rest is history, but what cannot be denied is that he always put the club first. Many a time he played outside-left when his

best position was definitely inside. He finally settled into the number nine shirt but playing as an inside forward, opening defences with his marvellous passing and always, still, having a terrific eye for a goal. His tally of championships and cups, an amazing England international career, being only one of two Englishmen to have won the European Cup and the World Cup, his great friend Nobby Stiles being the other, is envious, all recognised by the award of a Knighthood in 1994.'

Pos	Team	Pld	W	D	L	F	A	Pts
1	Liverpool	42	26	9	7	79	34	61
2	Leeds United	42	23	9	10	79	38	55
3	Burnley	42	24	7	11	79	47	55
4	Manchester United	42	18	15	9	84	59	51

Manchester United finally finished in fourth position in the league, with Liverpool winning the league and their Merseyside rivals Everton winning the FA Cup. The difference between United and Liverpool was ten points, but United had drawn 15 league matches this season so easy to see how draws turned into victories would have made a big difference. Bobby Charlton, along with Nobby Stiles and John Connelly still had football to play, the summer of 1966 was to see England stage the World Cup Finals and England would never have a better chance of winning it than at home...

Chapter Eight

WORLD CUP!

Summer 1966

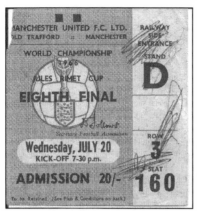

As World Cup fever intensified the question of hotel accommodation in Manchester arose, highlighting a difference between the Manchester of 1966 and now. While the famous Midland Hotel, where the Honourable Charles Rolls first met Sir Henry Royce in 1904, was and still is a prominent hotel, elsewhere in the city there was no comparison in 1966 to the number of hotel rooms now available in Manchester. Journalists alone, for example, needed 200 rooms in Manchester with up to 1,500 journalists expected to come to England for the tournament. To assist with the accommodation needs it was decided to use the University Halls of Residence in Fallowfield and also at the Manchester Technical College. Manchester United's Old Trafford stadium hosted three group matches, with tickets being available at £1-2-6d for standing and £6-6-0d for seating, not for ONE match but all THREE!

There would be four groups of four countries for the 16 competing nations in this eighth World Cup finals, with all the four previous tournament winners, Uruguay, Italy, Germany and Brazil competing. Brazil were in the group based in the North West along with Portugal, Bulgaria and Hungary but unlike the other three nations would not play a match at Old Trafford, playing all theirs at Goodison Park. They did though base themselves in Lymm close to where Bobby Charlton lived.

As was the custom at World Cups, the host nation, in this case, England of course, played the first tie. The match was against the first-ever winners of the trophy back in 1930, Uruguay, who had beat Argentina 4-2 in the final played in their capital Montevideo. In 1966 the first match was played in England's capital at Wembley Stadium on Monday 11 July 1966. Manchester United were well represented with Bobby Charlton, Nobby Stiles and John Connelly all in the starting line-up, but a well-disciplined Uruguay defence held firm. The match set a very low-key tone to start the competition ending 0-0 and disappointing the capacity crowd and the huge numbers now able to watch at home on television.

Ominously the following evening, two of the favourites alongside

England, West Germany and Brazil, started their group matches with emphatic victories, 5-0 for Germany against Switzerland, and 2-0 for reigning champions Brazil against Bulgaria at Goodison Park. Pele and Garrincha scoring for Brazil and a young, stylish midfielder called Franz Beckenbauer scoring twice in the West Germany rout.

England's manager Alf Ramsey was, surprisingly, still finalising his starting eleven, and after the opening draw, John Connelly would not feature again in the tournament. Southampton's Terry Paine took his place in the next England match against Mexico and was in turn replaced for the last group game against France by Liverpool's Ian Callaghan. In the Mexico match though, Ramsey's side settled into a better style and rhythm, thanks mainly to a very accomplished display by Bobby Charlton. Although having the number nine centre-forward shirt, Bobby oozed class in the midfield, gliding over the Wembley turf, scoring England's first goal of the tournament with a terrific shot and then seeing Roger Hunt settling the match, and a nation's nerves with the second goal.

Uruguay's 2-1 victory over France put a lot of pressure on the French side as they faced England in the last group match. Liverpool's Roger Hunt followed up his goal against Mexico by scoring twice to give England another comfortable 2-0 victory, marred slightly by an injury to Tottenham's Jimmy Greaves, one of the great goal scorers for both club and country, and an incident which saw Nobby Stiles cited by the French for a tackle on their inside-forward Jacques Simon. This reverberated for a few days as France demanded action was taken against Nobby, but Alf Ramsey was not going to let anybody take his relatively new-found defensive warrior away from his World Cup plans.

The main drama of the World Cup was played out in Groups Three and Four. Brazil in Group Three were heavily fancied to complete a trio of World Cup Final victories but were sensationally dethroned as they finished in third position of four, only recording their opening day victory over Bulgaria. Pele had faced some very strong tackling in that opening match and missed the game with Hungary when without him Brazil sensationally lost 3-1. Therefore, all the pressure was on Brazil when they faced Portugal in the final group match. Portugal, with a very strong foundation from a side Manchester United had come to know very well, Benfica, were a very dangerous opposition. On the night of the two famous number 10s, Eusebio and a returning Pele, it was Eusebio who won hands down as he scored twice in a 3-1 victory for his country that saw Brazil eliminated.

In Group Four unfancied North Korea achieved a remarkable victory over a strong Italian side in a match played at Middlesbrough's Ayresome Park. Their hero was Pak Doo Ik whose first-half goal won the match, which qualified North Korea and eliminated Italy! North Korea's award for this victory was a quarter-final at Goodison Park against Portugal. By half time the watching viewers across the world were amazed to see Korea going goal for goal with Portugal and leading 3-2 at half time. It took a virtuoso performance from Portugal's Eusebio, scoring four goals himself, to turn the match around for his country with a final score of 5-3.

All quarter-final matches were played on the same Saturday afternoon, 23 July 1966. The U.S.S.R (Union of Soviet Socialist Republics) beat Hungary 2-1 in a low-key match, West Germany continued to steam-roll their opposition beating Uruguay 4-0, the same side England had floundered against in the opening match of the competition. Portugal had, of course, finally won their incredible match with North Korea, which left England to face Argentine, a game which would turn out to be anything but low key!

Retraining their advantage of playing at Wembley Stadium, Alf Ramsey had finally settled on his desired eleven, which meant heartbreak for the great Jimmy Greaves who could not prove his fitness allowing West Ham United's Geoff Hurst to take his place. Ramsey also decided to abandon any wingers and brought back Blackpool's Alan Ball to occupy the right side with West Ham's Martin Peters the left side, with both playing in attacking and defensive roles as required. It was a day when physical and mental toughness would be required from all the England players as they had to endure severe provocation from Argentina, which eventually erupted when their captain, Antonio Rattin, a very imposing figure, was sent off by the diminutive West German referee Rudolf Kreitlein. The controversial dismissal occurred half-way through the first-half. It took an inordinate length of time for Rattin to leave the field of play. When he finally did, after at one point it looked likely that the whole Argentine side would follow him off in sympathy, it left a poisonous atmosphere on the pitch. A late goal from Geoff Hurst not only vindicated his selection in the team but also settled the quarter-final match and put England into their first-ever World Cup Semi-Final.

England's semi-final promised a very different match, and so it proved as Portugal came to Wembley Stadium and played their part in an excellent game worthy of the occasion. Probably the two most natural footballers on either side, Bobby Charlton and Eusebio, players who had opposed each other on occasions for their respective clubs, Manchester United and Benfica, dominated the game with Charlton's two goals exceeding Eusebio's one and delivering a World Cup Final appearance for England, the home of football, for the first time. West Germany overcame U.S.S.R, 2-1 at Goodison Park in the other semi-final to offer a mouth-watering World Cup Final.

The game took place on Saturday 30 July 1966 at Wembley Stadium when almost all of Britain not lucky enough to be amongst the capacity crowd seemed to be glued to the television. Well, that was less one Scotsman, with United's Denis Law famously taking himself off for a round of golf while the final took place!

Two of his club mates, Bobby Charlton and Nobby Stiles were at Wembley though. They took their proud place in the starting eleven, no substitutes, so there were a further eleven who had made the squad of 22 watching on the benches with manager Alf Ramsey and his coaches, trainers and medical people including the former Busby Babe Wilf McGuinness who was beginning to make his mark as a very fine coach.

Interestingly, there are two match programmes for this final. Firstly, the tournament issue which people could fill in as the games took place, and a second updated issue was produced on the day, as England were in the final, with all the games recorded and the pictures of both squads of 22 players from England and West Germany around the team line ups on the centre pages. Eight pages of picture action from the matches played were included at the expense of pre-tournament information. Both issues were 2/6 (13p) the original being of 68 pages, the final of 66 pages as the two blank sheets for notes were not now required.

England lost the toss to wear national colours and so wore red shirts and white shorts with West Germany in their traditional strip of white shirts and black shorts. The early exchanges saw Geoff Hurst test the nerve of the German goalkeeper Tilkowski by leaving him badly winded, but it was a defensive mistake by the normally so reliable Ray Wilson of Everton that led to the first goal. He headed the ball back towards the centre of play as opposed to away, and Helmut Haller drove the ball past Gordon Banks.

Being behind for the first time in the tournament did not appear to unsettle England though, and marvellous quick thinking by Captain Bobby Moore soon set up the equaliser. Moore quickly took a free-kick, floating it perfectly for his West Ham United club-mate Geoff Hurst to glide home a header. Twenty minutes played and 1-1. England dominated play from then on without really looking like scoring, and the match was still tied with less than 15 minutes left to play. One man who dominated all the game though, was England's youngest player, Alan Ball. He was just perpetual motion up and down the right side of play, and it was from one of his breaks that his cross went to Hurst to attempt a shot on goal. Hurst's effort was blocked by a West German defender; the ball looped up in the air to land perfectly at the feet of Martin Peters who smashed it home. England 2-1 in front and only 15 minutes plus any injury time left.

That injury time was to prove crucial though. West Germany were awarded a free-kick close to the penalty area, and the hard-driven shot by their left-winger Emmerich bounced off defenders to land at the feet of wing half Wolfgang Weber who scored from close range. As soon as England kicked off the final whistle went and as its blast was heard around the stadium, it now seemed possible that World Cup glory had eluded England. Alf Ramsey though had other ideas; he quickly seized the moment to remind his team of just how far they had come, there were to be no regrets, the World Cup was waiting there for them to win a second time this afternoon. Thankfully, the whole team responded, none more so than Alan Ball though whose running and drive had run the West Germany defenders ragged.

Ten minutes into extra time, it was Ball who provided the cross which Geoff Hurst turned against the crossbar and down over the goal line.

Or was it?!

Fifty-three years on, debate still rages as to if it crossed the line, but the men who mattered had no doubt, linesman Tofik Bakhramov from the U.S.S.R. flagged decisively that it had, and referee Gottfried Dienst from Switzerland whistled to say he agreed. Naturally, the West Germany players were livid, but the decision was made, and England led 3-2. As the second period of extra-time was winding down, and England supporters feared another late equaliser, Captain Bobby Moore showed incredible composure in his own area by looking up, moving the ball further along with his foot and then playing an inch-perfect pass for Geoff Hurst to control, run on and hammer home. Cue scenes of delirium and the knowledge that England had won the World Cup, which has not been achieved again 53 years later. Indeed, it looks likely it will be another 53 years on before it will happen again!

The England side that brought this glory to the nation (although Prime Minister Harold Wilson did try to inform people that it was his leadership of the country that had delivered it!) was as follows; Gordon Banks (Leicester City) George Cohen (Fulham) Ray Wilson (Everton) Nobby Stiles (Manchester United) Jack Charlton (Leeds United) Bobby Moore (West Ham United and Captain) Alan Ball (Blackpool) Roger Hunt (Liverpool) Bobby Charlton (Manchester United) Geoff Hurst (West Ham United) and Martin Peters (West Ham United).

Managed by Alf Ramsey, these footballers are immortalised, justly so, remembered for a brilliant display of teamwork, punctuated by high-class skill in all the vital areas of goalkeeper, defence, midfield and attack. Alf Ramsey though was the mastermind, totally single-minded as to what was required and who delivered what he often promised: *'England will win the World Cup.'*

Chapter Nine

CHAMPIONS AGAIN!

1966-67

As we have seen, the summer of 1966 saw England, once again, become the centre of the football world. It was the centre of youth culture too with the Beatles and the Rolling Stones riding high in the charts on both sides of the Atlantic. Having changed music forever August would see the last ever public performance by the Beatles at Candlestick Park in Los Angeles. International politics was dominated by the Vietnam War with 32 arrests being made outside the US Embassy in London when an anti-war protest turned violent. The 60s had seen many challenges to social norms. Things didn't always happen quickly though, and sometimes they came about through struggle. In July 1966 West Indian-born Asquith Xavier was appointed as a guard at Euston railway station after the opposition of the local staff committee was overturned, ending a colour bar in Euston Station that is rumoured to have been in place for the last 12 years. At the same time the sitcom *Till Death Us Do Part* started its first series on BBC1. Alf Garnett brilliantly played by Warren Mitchell reflecting the reactionary element in the white working-class whose beliefs are challenged by his daughter's 'scouse git' layabout husband, Mike Rawlins (Tony Booth). The days when black players would be fully accepted in top-flight football were still a long way off. Indeed, it is sad to report that in 2019, an undercurrent of racism has reappeared in football after it had looked like the problem had been eliminated.

Manchester United were the embodiment of football and youth culture. Their 1966-67 season started with a period of uncertainty. As they had finished fourth the previous season, they were one position off qualifying for the Inter-Cities Fairs Cup but could still have been given a place if a European side dropped out. In the event, this didn't happen, but the lateness of the World Cup Final, 30 July 1966 had given no time whatsoever for such as Bobby Charlton, Nobby Stiles and John Connelly to rest. Indeed, with all three going on the pre-season tour to Vienna, Munich and a far from friendly match in Glasgow against Celtic, it left precious little time to prepare before the season started.

The Celtic match had given a fired up Scottish side opportunity to knock an English club off any perch they may be on after the country's World Cup success. From United's point of view, it was arranged as a pre-season friendly, but the packed Celtic Park soon brought that idea to an end. Celtic were a very fine side, and their 4-1 victory would be a prelude from which they would go on and become Britain's first European Cup winners at the end of this season...

The opening day of the new league season saw a visit from West Bromwich Albion and a goal feast in a 5-3 victory for the 41,343 crowd. The attendance was surprisingly small, given the euphoria of winning the World Cup was expected to bring crowds flocking back to the game. As it turned out, it would be the smallest of the season though, as United played some excellent exciting football, befitting a side containing forwards such as they possessed. One of the three United World Cup heroes was on the score sheet in that first match, not the expected ones of Charlton or Connelly but it was Nobby Stiles who scored a rare goal, along with a welcome return goal from George Best after his injury, two from Denis Law and one from David Herd.

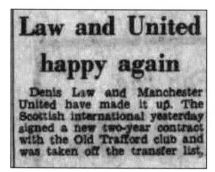

Law and United happy again

Denis Law and Manchester United have made it up. The Scottish international yesterday signed a new two-year contract with the Old Trafford club and was taken off the transfer list.

Denis had been in the news during the summer as he had wanted a pay increase, but Matt Busby was not for moving, and the brilliant Lawman was quickly put on the transfer list, although thankfully only for a short time. Mind you, it could have been Denis fretting about what England might, and then did do in the World Cup Finals, indeed, on the day of the final he went playing golf!

Showing his vital importance to Manchester United, it was Denis's two goals that earned a 2-1 win at the always difficult Goodison Park home of Everton. Just over a week later United scored an even more convincing win beating Everton 3-0 at Old Trafford. A match that was marred when trouble broke out in the Stretford End at half-time. Everton fans had taken their place at the front of the Stretford End but the days when home and away fans could happily mingle were coming to an end. The following day's Guardian reported that *'Six people were taken to hospital suffering from serious injuries and several arrests were made after fighting broke out amongst the crowd of 61,000 ... Police and ambulancemen worked into the second-half treating the casualties behind the goal and trying to break up the fighting. Dozens of spectators were treated for minor injuries and hundreds were helped to safety. A St John Ambulance spokesman said the fist aid room had been like a battlefield all night.'*

Despite these victories, United had an indifferent start to the season with four victories and three defeats from the first seven games. A fourth defeat came in United's return to the League Cup competition for only the second time in its existence when struggling Blackpool hammered them 5-1 at Bloomfield Road. Even allowing for the fact that Denis Law and Bobby Charlton missed the game, it was a very poor performance. Matt Busby reacted immediately by breaking the record transfer for a goalkeeper for the third time in his Manchester United managerial career (Reg Allen and Harry Gregg the other two) by signing Londoner Alex Stepney from Chelsea for over £50,000. He also allowed John Connelly to join Blackburn Rovers ending a two-year stay at Old Trafford in which John had proved a very fine and reliable player. He had played every game in United's 64-65 season, and only Charlton and Crerand had played more during 65-66. While John's departure was surprising, the emergence of his replacement John Aston was yet again a sign of Matt Busby's trust of his emerging young players.

Alex Stepney's debut was right in at the deep end as United played Manchester City for the first time in the league since City's relegation in 1962-63. The United Review for this match broke with tradition in the centre-page team line-up, instead of reflecting the sides in a 1-2-3-5 formation they listed them 1-11 with Alex Stepney the new number one. A single Denis Law goal settled the match in United's favour. Alex Stepney had a memorable day as he explained to Roy Cavanagh.

'I had started my career with Tooting & Mitcham before joining Millwall. There were some great times at The Den, and I was sorry to leave them in 1966 just after the World Cup. A move to West Ham United had fallen through before Tommy Docherty, then at Chelsea, signed me. Evidentially, Joe Mears the Chelsea Chairman had told Tommy to get rid of Peter Bonetti, so he bought me as the replacement. Soon after, Joe Mears died suddenly, and Tommy decided to keep Bonetti at Chelsea, and I was on my way again.'

Alex only managed one appearance at Chelsea, but his reputation as an outstanding goalkeeper had spread north, so when Matt Busby decided he needed a goalkeeper as the last piece in another championship jigsaw, Alex Stepney was the number one choice. Tommy Docherty and Alex's paths would cross again at Manchester United. Within days of his signing he was playing against City as he continued his conversation with Roy;

'Even though I was a Londoner born and bred, the chance of signing for Manchester United was too good to turn down. No sooner had I signed for United than I was playing against City at Old Trafford in my debut. 63,000 turned up to give me a quick taste of the atmosphere that I was going to become accustomed to. We beat City 1-0 thanks to a goal from Denis Law and I was involved in the chase for the League Championship!'

Notably, of the 11 who played against City, only Alex, Pat Crerand, Tony Dunne and Denis Law had cost a transfer fee with the other seven players all coming through the Manchester United youth system. United's victory kept them in the cluster of clubs chasing the top spot. Only two points separated the top ten clubs, and a visit from Burnley gave United not only their second home fixture running but a chance to establish themselves at the top. Another of the small group of players United had bought, David Herd, returned from injury against Burnley and was one of the scorers in a 4-1 victory.

The following week saw the same scoreline - only this time against United, in the away match at Nottingham Forest. Despite the defeat, the match was a turning point for United. A string of poor away performances were threatening to end all hopes of another championship. Another youngster, Bobby Noble, came back into the side replacing Shay Brennan at full-back. The change seemed to have an instant effect with a 2-1 victory at Blackpool who had beaten United 5-1 only a month earlier

On Friday 21 October 1966 a most tragic incident happened in the South Wales town of Aberfan as a result of a colliery spoil tip, which flowed at high speed down into the town killing 144 people, including 116 school children between the ages of seven and ten. The whole nation was in mourning for such a heart-breaking disaster.

THE BEST OF BEST

IT was one of those moments that not even the tricks of memory can polish into something more marvellous

It was there to see, to savour, to enthuse over —the genius of George Best, Manchester United's Irish international.

For seconds that must have seemed an age to Chelsea full back Eddie McCreadie, he was still, his body keeled over at an incredible angle, his right foot poised like a wand over the ball.

Then Best was away, sprinting for a return to the pass he had stabbed to the feet of David Sadler.

An incredible shot, hit off the wrong foot, swept past a bewildered Peter

GEORGE BEST . . . United's Beatle-cut genius made the match his own.

At the beginning of November, another away victory came. This time at the then top of the table Chelsea, despite their sluggish start United were now most definitely in the running for the title. A capacity crowd of 56,000 where it was reported over 60,000 programmes were sold, saw George Best take the opportunity to put on a show for his admiring public. London became particularly enchanted with this young genius of a footballer. The Chelsea ground is just beside the famous Kings Road, and along with Carnaby Street in central London, it was becoming the place to be seen due to its fashion offerings. George became attracted to all these places whenever he had time off from playing football. His image had outgrown the game of football itself it seemed at times. He did not forget his footballing skills at Stamford Bridge though, as he scored and set up John Aston for one of his two goals as United won 3-1 to go top of the table, it was another performance by George to light up London.

The full-house at Chelsea was indicative of all Manchester United away matches this season, and indeed most seasons of that period. Manchester United proved to be the most popular visitors for home supporters. Mind you; this was a truly star-studded side now that it also included a record signing for a goalkeeper in Alex Stepney. In front of Stepney, the bedrock of the team included two English World Cup winners in Bobby Charlton and Nobby Stiles, along with the rock of a centre-half Bill Foulkes. Three outstanding Scottish players were in the line-up: Pat Crerand, David Herd and the charismatic Denis Law. Ireland too was represented through one of United's greatest full-backs in Tony Dunne and the other Irishman who happened to be a genius of a footballer in Georgie Best. The other players who appeared this season more than ten times were three of England's most promising young players in David Sadler, John Aston and Bobby Noble, plus an English born Shay Brennan. Brennan, who made history in 1965 when he became the first player born outside Ireland to represent the country.

To show the effect on attendances, the average for Manchester United home matches increased dramatically from 39,000 to 54,726 with the lowest the opening match against West Bromwich Albion to a highest later in the season when Nottingham Forest came for a top of the table match which drew 62,727. As was the continued fascination with the FA Cup, both home matches versus Stoke City and Second Division Norwich City drew capacity 63,000 attendances. The size of these crowds began to show in Manchester United's now healthy finances. Remember, at the start of the decade United were in a financially precarious position, now the figures for 1965 had shown a pre-tax profit of nearly £115,000, which would be worth over £2 million in 2019.

As was noted earlier in this book, Wilf McGuinness had the misfortune of breaking his leg in 1959, ending a hugely promising playing career at just 22 years old. Wilf was already an England international, and no doubt would have won many national and international honours. He was in demand off the pitch, going on to coach Manchester United's reserves and being included as one of Alf Ramsey's backroom staff for the 1966 World Cup. Wilf though always had this desire to give playing another opportunity, with Matt Busby only too willing to give him a chance. So, a return to reserve level it was for Wilf, and a scoring one at that, against Sheffield United where another youngster made a big impression, Brian Kidd, scoring a hat-trick. Sadly, for Wilf, his comeback only lasted the season before he had to admit defeat, but he continued to be a vital part of Manchester United's coaching staff.

When Sunderland arrived at Old Trafford at the end of November 1966, it provided an incredible occurrence with United's David Herd scoring four goals in United's 5-0 victory, but against three goalkeepers! The first was against the regular Sunderland keeper Jim Montgomery before he was injured, then he scored against the first replacement centre-half, Charlie Hurley. Now in the age of substitutes, Sunderland decided to bring on John Parke to take over the green jersey, although he was an outfield player, they felt he would be the most comfortable in the net. In the second-half though, he was beaten twice by David Herd who therefore completed his memorable afternoon.

Herd was in fine form and bagged another hat-trick at West Bromwich Albion in a 4-3 win before Christmas as United moved towards 1967 as league leaders. A man who would not pick up a winner's medal if United won the title was Harry Gregg, as in December 1966 he left Old Trafford to join the Manchester United exodus to Stoke City alongside Dennis Viollet and Maurice Setters. While we have covered a lot of Harry's career in this book, there are still not enough words to express the gratitude of all Manchester United supporters for what the great man did for the club.

Harold Wilson was a shrewd politician who knew how to win popular appeal. Many believe the timing of his call for an early election drew on the wave of optimism in the country on the eve of England's hosting of the World Cup. Wilson fought and won a notable battle with the establishment over the award of the New Year's Honours for 1967. Honours had traditionally been reserved for the great and the good amongst the political classes. Wilson had first broken with tradition when honouring Stanley Matthews in 1965 this time he awarded knighthoods to Alf Ramsey and an OBE to Bobby Moore. Into 1967, the football world bestowed an honour to Bobby Charlton who was named European Footballer of the year only the second Englishman to be so honoured after Stanley Matthews who had been the very first winner of the award. Scotsman Denis Law had, of course, won this in 1964. United now had two European Footballers of the year in their side. A rare feat indeed and one that would be extended further.

January 15, 1967, saw the first-ever Super Bowl in America with the Green Bay Packers beating the Kansas Chiefs 35-10 in Los Angeles. The week after, Manchester had its version of a super bowl as in their first match of the New Year, crossed the city to play their neighbours at Maine Road. The 1-1 draw marked the beginning of a pattern of what was regarded as the perfect combination for title-chasers - winning your home league matches and drawing away from home. From this match on, until the title was decided, Manchester United would win all their home games and draw their away fixtures. Interestingly, for the last two matches, it was reversed!

FA Cup matches, as noted earlier meant huge crowds, and so it was as Stoke City arrived in early January at Old Trafford. Continuing his love of the competition, Denis Law scored one of United's goals in the 2-0 victory which earned a 4th round tie at home to Second Division Norwich City.

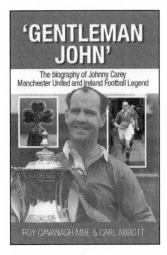

Back into league action, a top of the table match with Nottingham Forest highlighted just how successful Johnny Carey was as a manager. In 2018 Carl Abbott and Roy Cavanagh penned an acclaimed biography on Carey's tremendous career. Not only was he one of Manchester United's greatest ever footballers and captains, but he was also Ireland's. After his playing career finished, he had real success at all the clubs he managed, Blackburn Rovers, Everton, Leyton Orient and Nottingham Forest, and again also as the Ireland manager. The title of our book summed him up perfectly, 'Gentleman John'.

Carey's Forest side, with the support of his assistant and future United favourite, Tommy Cavanagh, were United's main rivals for the title. A full house at Old Trafford saw a late, brilliant goal by Denis Law decide the match to put Manchester United firmly at the top of the table. The report by Eric Todd in the following Monday's Guardian provides a perfect testimony to the brilliance of Denis Law:

'On this day when distinction was distributed so evenly and so generously it was almost impertinent to push anyone to the front. An exception nevertheless must be made of Law. He has written at least two autobiographies. Whatever facts modesty insisted that he omit have been reported many times, and in many languages, His skill has exhausted all superlatives. Against Forest he hovered and when Law hovers, some team is going to suffer, sometimes by way of variation in the middle. Hovering. Then someone—usually Charlton or Crerand—delivered a long pass or a short one. There was a flash of red and Law was away. And Forest's defenders, all first-class men, could do nothing to stop him. I have no idea what Law proposes to do with his life when, to-the relief of his opponents, he retires from football. He would have made a splendid highwayman, he is a second Scarlet Pimpernel, he could be another Raffles. Maybe some police force will invite him to give lectures on breaking and entering or on loitering with intent. In the nicest and most lawful way, of course.'

It was now five years since Pat Crerand had joined Manchester United from Glasgow Celtic and his trophy haul of FA Cup and League Championship winner made an impressive collection. His displays this season were certainly a major part of Manchester United's chances of increasing their trophy count. That respected journalist Arthur Walmsley certainly noted Pat Crerand's influence and commented that *'When Crerand plays well, United play well'* a comment that would last throughout Pat's Manchester United career.

When playing with relatively small squads as sides did in the 1960s, the question of whether it was possible to be successful in more than one competition was ever-present. Spurs in 1961 were the only team to achieve the double that decade, and despite their talent, United's double campaign ended with a surprise, even sensational, 2-1 defeat in the 4th round of the FA Cup at home to Second Division Norwich City. The defeat did have the bonus of allowing the club to concentrate fully on winning the League Championship again, and then perhaps give Matt Busby a final chance of lifting his dream of winning the European Cup.

The away match at Arsenal was switched from the normal Saturday afternoon to a Friday night at Highbury Stadium because the Football League wanted to give the Final of their League Cup full prominence in London on the Saturday, oh how times have changed! Manchester United came up with the innovative idea of beaming the match live by closed-circuit TV back to Old Trafford. Over 28,000 turned up to watch the action from Highbury on the big screens, while 63,000 were in London watching the live-action as Arsenal and United drew 1-1. The Football League Cup Final incidentally, the first time it had been played as one match instead of home and away, saw Third Division Queens Park Rangers, coming from 2-0 down, to beat West Bromwich Albion 3-2 at Wembley Stadium.

David Herd had missed a possible return to his old Arsenal club as he had an injury but was fit to return the following week at Old Trafford for the visit of Leicester City, sadly with disastrous results for this very fine centre-forward only two minutes into the match as he recalled to Roy Cavanagh.

'I took a pass from Denis Law at the scoreboard end of Old Trafford on the edge of the Leicester City penalty area and remember my shot passing goalkeeper Gordon Banks into the net just as Graham Cross the Leicester left half crashed into me quite accidentally. Straight away though I knew it was a leg break.'

The injury did not stop Manchester United going on to win 5-2 to stay top of the table, but there was concern over David Herd and to how his absence could affect United's title challenge, particularly as the next opponent was away at the main challenger at that time - Liverpool. That was also Easter Saturday and set up three matches in four days with home and away games with Fulham to follow. The absence of David Herd though gave David Sadler the chance of an extended run in the side, back in the position where he had made his debut back in 1963, that of centre-forward. David had made real progress at United since then, becoming a more than useful centre-half and left-half when needed. In future years he would also fill the inside-left position and become an unsung hero of Manchester United. His inclusion in the side also meant that Manchester United had four members of their 1964 FA Youth Cup winning side playing regularly in their first team three years on, those being Bobby Noble, George Best, John Aston and David Sadler.

Despite the fixture congestion and the difficulty of their opponents, United continued their sequence of away draws and home victories, drawing 0-0 at Liverpool and 2-2 at Fulham and then beating the London side 2-1 at home. When another London side, West Ham United containing three World Cup winners in captain Bobby Moore, hat-trick hero of the final Geoff Hurst, and scorer of the other goal in that final, Martin Peters, were comfortably beaten 2-0 at Old Trafford the title was becoming Manchester United's to lose.

The next two Saturdays though saw both of United's fixtures cancelled for different reasons. Saturday the 8th saw their league opponents Sheffield Wednesday still in the FA Cup and playing away at Chelsea, which put United's visit to Hillsborough back until the Tuesday. Then, the following Saturday saw the England v Scotland international at Wembley meaning United could cancel their league game with Southampton until the Tuesday as Bobby Charlton and Nobby Stiles were in the England side and Denis Law in the Scotland team. Roy Cavanagh went to both Hillsborough and Wembley and still has a vivid memory of the two occasions.

'I went to Sheffield with a couple of work colleagues, and you knew straight away as you got near to the ground the crowd was going to be huge. Cars were left on the side of the road at all angles, and we just abandoned ours and made a dash for the turnstiles. Struggling to get into any form of a queue the entering was climbing over the actual turnstile and then being faced with incredible swaying and being crushed which left me with memories of the incident at the Tottenham match I mentioned back in 1961. It was all, sadly, a foretaste of what would happen at the same Leppings Lane end with the disaster at the Liverpool v Nottingham Forest semi-final of 1989 when 96 people were crushed to death. In the match, two great goals by Bobby Charlton seemed to have given Manchester United a comfortable victory until two equally fine goals from Sheffield Wednesday pulled the match back for yet another away draw.'

Roy then went to London for the weekend of the Home International between England and Scotland with the Scots wanting to prove that a victory would make them World Champions!

The scenes around and inside Wembley Stadium for this international were amazing. Everywhere you looked there were Scottish people swaying as they walked, leaning out of taxis with their 'we are the people' mantra which I remember from a couple of years back. Inside requests from women could they climb on your back to get a better view and a very warm day contributed to an interesting afternoon! Scotland were led magnificently by Denis Law who was simply superb, although injury to centre-half Jack Charlton did not help England's cause. Law put Scotland one-nil up which Bobby Lennox increased before a struggling Jack Charlton, playing as a centre-forward pulled a goal back. A late goal from Jim McCalliog settled the Scotland victory, although Geoff Hurst scored a very late consolation. Scotland were brilliant, and the victory over the current World Cup holders immediately had everyone around claiming that title had gone north! Oh, they also took the goalposts and most of the pitch with them as well!'

After a victory in the rearranged home fixture against Southampton, United continued their pattern of winning at home and drawing away by taking a point in a 0-0 draw at Sunderland. Later that day though an incident was to have a disastrous effect on the career of that excellent full-back Bobby Noble. After the team had returned to Old Trafford by coach, Bobby took the short journey home to Sale by car and suffered extensive injuries when his car crashed, leaving Bobby unconscious for three days in a critical condition. He was only 21 at the time, and although in future he would make a recovery from the injuries, his attempts to recover full fitness were unsuccessful, and he never played the game again.

April 1967 had seen the 100/1 outsider Foinavon win the Grand National when his opponents fell, refused or were hampered or brought down in a mêlée at the 23rd fence – since renamed the 'Foinavon fence'. By the end of April as a future United manager would once remark – it would have taken United to do a 'Devon Loch' for them to lose their grip on the championship. They had no intention of doing so and the chance to clinch the 1967 First Division title was firmly in Manchester United's grasp when they travelled to Upton Park, home of West Ham United on the first Saturday of May 1967. Roy Cavanagh recalled the emotional and very hectic day. *'As with the recent match at Sheffield Wednesday, the atmosphere around and inside the ground was electric. Thousands wanting to see the match, not all ticket, meant similar scenes as Hillsborough with crushing and swaying all over the place, and that was outside the ground! Inside there was no room to move yet somehow, bottles were thrown by West Ham fans up to the roof of the stand with the glass cascading down onto all the United fans. It was very hostile, to say the least, but on the field, Manchester United were 4-0 up by the 25th minute thanks to goals from Bobby Charlton, George Best and the unlikely duo of Pat Crerand and Bill Foulkes. The title was in the bag and the Manchester United fans, me included, were in a very happy, party mood. Two second-half goals from Denis Law completed a 6-1 victory. As we crawled back to the tube, I bumped into a former schoolteacher who was already making a mark as an artist, Harold Riley a long-standing United fan and we had a great end to a brilliant day.'*

Describing the match in Sunday's Observer, Bob Ferrier had no doubt where this performance placed Manchester United and their 'red and white ragamuffin battalions':

'A monumental performance by Manchester United confirmed them their

championship, virtually obliterated West Ham and left London with the marvellously concluding statement from Matt Busby's team, that if the capital is to have the cup final, Manchester is once again the centre of the universe. For the ragged red and white ragamuffin battalions that invaded the field at the end, screaming for Busby, there had never been any doubt about that'.

While the football had been beautiful, scenes off the pitch had become notably ugly. As Roy Cavanagh recalled bottles were thrown to the roof of the stands as West Ham fans objected to the United fan's taunts of 'United are champions'. The Sunday People reported that 30 people were treated in hospital after the game.

The league trophy was presented at the last game of the season, at home to Stoke City in a 0-0 draw. The presentation marked the seventh time Manchester United had won the league title, and the euphoria was so great that nobody, but nobody would have realised that Manchester United, now the *'centre of the football universe'*, would have to wait another 26 years for their next title win…….

Pos	Club	Pld	W	D	L	GF	GA	Pts
1	Manchester United	42	24	12	6	84	45	60
2	Nottingham Forest	42	23	10	9	64	41	56
3	Tottenham Hotspur	42	24	8	10	71	48	56

Four days after the Stoke City match, Manchester United embarked on a ground-breaking tour of Australia and New Zealand, also returning to play a couple of matches in the United States where they had toured a couple of times before. Twelve matches were arranged and flying off as Champions made the trip even sweeter, with another crack at the European Cup to be had the following season. The cost to watch Manchester United play in that top club competition would range from £8-10-0d (£8-50p) to £12-10-0d (£12-50p) for a season ticket and £8-18-6d (£8.93p) to £13-2-6d (£13-13p) for a recently introduced League Match Ticket Book.

On the 25th May 1967, while Manchester United were thousands of miles away, Glasgow Celtic became the first British club to win the European Cup, when they beat former champions Inter Milan of Italy 2-1 in Lisbon. The match which has never been forgotten by many people, least of all some Celts fans who left for Lisbon and decided to stay there they were so excited by the result!. The team were labelled the 'Lisbon Lions' for their historic achievement. Later in the year, the beautiful city of Lisbon suffered terribly from floods with over 450 people killed.

A day after Glasgow Celtic's memorable victory, the Beatles released their album 'Sgt Pepper's Lonely Heart Club Band' in England which is still today, looked back as a memorable piece of music, and with an iconic cover, an album which lasted 27 weeks at number one in the Album chart.

It was another example of how popular music was evolving during the Swinging Sixties, which Britain most certainly was in 1967.

The month of June 1967 saw a terrible six-day war concerning Israel's difference with other Middle East nations, Egypt, Syria, Iraq and Jordan, while a tragic air disaster occurred in Stockport as a plane, returning to Manchester from Palma carrying 72 people, crashed into open land close to the town centre.

Chapter Ten

THE HOLY GRAIL - EUROPEAN CUP WINNERS

1967-68

It was only fitting that in June 1967 colour was introduced into mainstream BBC2 television programmes, starting with the coverage of the Wimbledon Tennis tournament, as colour was no doubt in everybody's lives now. In May 1968, colour was most definitely in Manchester United, fan's lives. After three failed attempts to win the European Cup over the previous 12 years, the second of which ended in tragedy for one of football's greatest ever sides, the holy grail was finally reached on a glorious night at Wembley. This is how they got there...

As champions again for the seventh time, Manchester United competed pre-season for the Charity Shield, an event in which they had lots of history. They were, in fact, the first winners of the shield back in 1908 when as First Division champions they played the Southern League champions, Queens Park Rangers at Stamford Bridge, home of Chelsea. A 1-1 draw took the clubs back the following week, and this time United won 4-0. Three years later United recorded the, still, highest score in a Charity Shield match, beating Swindon Town 8-4. Those results were the start of their record today in 2019 as the most successful side in Charity Shield history with 17 outright wins, and four shares, one of which came in this 1967 season against Tottenham Hotspur.

These two clubs have produced many a memorable match over the years, and this was no exception as the match included an amazing goal by the Tottenham goalkeeper Pat Jennings! He was one of the many famous names in the Tottenham side, Jimmy Greaves, Mike England, Terry Venables, Dave MacKay, Alan Mullery as well as Pat. Manchester United, of course, had their own stars, none brighter anywhere in the game than Bobby Charlton, Denis Law and George Best, while yet another youngster off the famous conveyor belt of talent, Brian Kidd, made his United debut.

Tottenham were already one goal up when after just eight minutes Pat Jennings had his incredible moment as a goal scorer as opposed to goal stopper to put Spurs two up. Let us hear what the goalkeeper at the other end that day, Alex Stepney had to say about it when he gave Roy Cavanagh an interview. *'We were already one down when Pat from the Stretford End penalty area, conscious of a new rule for goalkeepers was concentrating on kicking the ball as far down the pitch as possible. Unfortunately for me, it was such a mighty kick that on a rain-soaked pitch it reared like a cricket bouncer and went right over my head into the net. It was just one of those things, and I had just to get over it and concentrate on the game.'*

Bobby Charlton then took over the game, scoring two spectacular long-range goals. The second of which put a devastating finish to a dazzling run by Law and a sharp pass by Kidd and is immortalised through the memorable commentary of Kenneth Wolstenholme as *'a goal good enough to win the League, the Cup, the Charity Shield, the World Cup and even the Grand National!* '. With a further goal for each side, it left the match drawn at 3-3 and both sides sharing the trophy for six months each.

Mid-week an unusual friendly took place at Old Trafford with a full Manchester United side playing the Italian Olympic Xl with two Manchester lads from Collyhurst, both from the same St Patrick's school, World Cup hero Nobby Stiles and young Brian Kidd on his second United appearance, scoring the goals in a 2-0 victory.

A sluggish start in the league, which included an emphatic 3-1 opening day defeat at Everton, made Matt Busby make a change at full-back, giving a young Scottish lad, Francis Burns his debut in place of Shay Brennan at West Ham United. Francis, therefore, became the second debutant of the season, a further three would follow, and in Francis' case, it certainly helped as United won 3-1 at West Ham. The result gave everyone the chance to congratulate Matt Busby, who was already a CBE, on the news that he had been made the 66th Freeman of the City of Manchester.

A string of draws preceded the return of the European Cup to Old Trafford with a visit from Hibernians FC of Malta. The island which had been honoured with the George Cross for its bravery and heroism in the Second World War is also the home to one of the most famous fan clubs in the world, the Manchester United supporters club founded in 1959 and still going strong in 2019. A comfortable 4-0 victory for United would provide the needed insurance when they saw the state of the grassless pitch for the second leg!

Before that, Tottenham Hotspur made their second visit of the season to Old Trafford, where the crowd witnessed an amazing display from Denis Law, fully justifying his title as the *'King of Old Trafford'*. Firstly Denis scored one of his trademark overhead kicks only for the referee to disallow the goal. He then missed a penalty before he put United in front at 2-1 with a third goal from George Best (his second of the game) sealing a fine victory as Manchester United made it into the top five, and prepared to visit all their fans in Malta for the European Cup second leg match.

Despite the lovely warmth of Malta's weather and the welcome of their supporters, the hard grassless pitch made this a more difficult match than had been anticipated. That the game finished 0-0 was probably a surprise to many, but given the situation, the result suited everybody really and put Manchester United into the next round of the competition they desperately wanted to win for their manager, Matt Busby.

Back home, it was across the City of Manchester to play local rivals City at Maine Road. Now in their second season back in the First Division, there was no doubt that the City managerial team of flamboyant Malcolm Allison and the very well-liked and admired Joe Mercer, had no intention of letting Manchester City drop down the league again. A capacity crowd saw City take the lead, but Bobby Charlton scored two excellent goals to give United the bragging rights. On the same day as this match, Saturday 30 September 1967, radio in Britain was transformed by the re-structuring of the BBC programmes. Radio 1 became the home of popular music, Radio 2 of light music, Radio 3 was the home of cultural programmes while Radio 4 was the new station for the Home Service.

For the fourth time in his Manchester United career, in the match against Arsenal at Old Trafford Denis Law was sent off. This time it was fighting with fellow Scottish international Ian Ure, and both were sent for an early bath! The managers of the two sides appeared, publicly at least, to take a differing view on the altercation. Arsenal's manager, Bertie Mee, defended Ian Ure saying that *'If you want players that don't create problems you don't win anything'*. Matt Busby meanwhile kept his counsel but called players to a Monday morning meeting to emphasise that the players should *'behave like champions at all times'*. United took the points in a 1-0 win which kept them near the top of the table, convincing victories at Sheffield United (3-0) and home to Coventry City (4-0) consolidated their position. As a result of the sending-off, Denis Law was given another lengthy suspension, and there were also real concerns with his recurring knee problems, in total Law missed nine matches including both legs of the next European Cup tie against the Yugoslav champions Sarajevo.

Before his suspension started, Denis was in the United team which lost their first match since the opening day of the season, when a (still) record crowd of 49,946 at the City Ground, home of Nottingham Forest, saw United lose 3-1. While Denis was able to play; United had severe injury problems with Tony Dunne, Bill Foulkes and Nobby Stiles all missing. The injuries gave a young full-back, Frank Kopel his debut with other youngsters Brian Kidd, David Sadler, John Fitzpatrick, Francis Burns and, of course, George Best also playing that day.

During October and November 1967 two decisions were taken, which would have a profound effect on people and politics in Great Britain. Firstly, on 27 October the Abortion Bill was passed by Parliament with a month later on the 27 November, for the second time, France President Charles de Gaulle, vetoed the British application to join the European Economic Community, citing that the links Britain had with the Commonwealth and America would have an adverse effect on Europe. Interesting comparing matters of 2019 with the Brexit issue now eternally in the news.

Staying with Europe, Manchester United's next opponents were

Sarajevo, a city which will forever be etched into history because of the First World War. There on the 28th June 1914, Archduke Franz Ferdinand of the Austro-Hungarian Empire was assassinated by an 18-year Serbian which activated the simmering tensions in that part of the world, leading Germany and then Britain to become involved, starting one of the bloodiest conflicts imaginable.

Manchester United embarked on their first big charter flight since the fateful 6th February 1958 journey from Munich, as they travelled to Yugoslavia. The first part of the journey was fine, but the airport was in Dubrovnik some 160 miles from Sarajevo and involved a long coach journey. Then the opposition proved to be particularly difficult to break down and a second 0-0 away result in the European Cup ensued. The magic of the name Manchester United was seen by the hundreds packing the streets near the team's hotel and then the several thousand who turned up to see the side train. In later years, full back Tony Dunne, pictured above, said to Roy Cavanagh, *'I remember seeing a poster saying Sarajevo v Manchester United, in brackets Charlton, Law and Best etc., and saying to the team "there I am, Mr etc!"'* Anybody who saw Tony Dunne play would know he was far from an extra, indeed at this time one of the greatest full-backs in the world, either in a right or left-back position.

There were only two weeks between the ties, as we were still in the times when the competing clubs agreed on the dates, but this 1967-68 season brought an innovation to the tournament - that of away goals being counted as double. Although, a bit like the use (or none use!) of VAR it was only used in this round, and the quarter-finals onwards would revert to a third match and then a toss of the coin! For the return leg in Manchester, United were still without Denis Law, and it was George Best that took the eye in this match. He certainly took the Sarajevo players' eye as they continually kicked him in what was a very physical match indeed. George mind you, knew how to look after himself and sometimes got the first kick in which certainly turned the temperature up in front of a capacity Old Trafford crowd. What also did not help the Sarajevo players' minds was the Manchester United second goal which did seem to have been hooked back from over the deadline by John Aston for George Best to firmly hammer the ball home. Ten minutes from time though, Sarajevo scored, and nobody seemed to understand this new rule of away goals, not completely realising another Sarajevo goal would have meant a European Cup exit.

The ceremony for Matt Busby's award as Freeman of Manchester took place at Manchester Town Hall towards the end of November 1967 with the 'United Review' club programme on 2 December 1967 featuring this event and also announcing that for the first time, a Prime Minister would be in attendance for the match against West Bromwich Albion that day. That was Harold Wilson, who in his four years in the role had arranged the Knighthood for two footballers, and also claimed that the England World Cup win of 1966 was due to his leadership!

The day after this match, over 8,000 miles away from Manchester in South Africa, Professor Christian Barnard performed the first heart transplant. Sadly, the recipient only lived for 18 days, but now over 5,000 transplants a year are completed successfully all over the world.

As we have already seen attitudes and behaviour at football matches had deteriorated during the 1960s. Activities that began as harmless but irritating such as throwing toilet rolls at the opposing goalkeepers with some trying to throw as far as possible onto the pitch had developed into more serious vandalism and hooliganism. Vandalism of trains, especially the football specials that ferried supporters to away matches, had become widespread. For United's away match at Newcastle United on Saturday 9 December 1967, the special train from Manchester to Newcastle was cancelled. The supporters missed a fine match with a last-minute equaliser from the unlikely source of full-back Tony Dunne earning a 2-2 draw to keep United top of the table. The match programme for this game carried an insert, in the form of a 24-page match magazine called '*Football League Review*'. The review had become a feature of most match programmes, providing informative coverage of all four leagues.

The much-needed return of Denis Law the week after against Everton, put United in a strong position as Christmas approached. Denis, as was his style, simply walked back into the team as though the previous seven weeks had not happened and turned in a virtuoso performance creating United's second goal and then scoring the third to reverse the 3-1 defeat at Everton on the opening day of the season.

Christmas Day football had ended in England back in 1957, Manchester United incidentally beating Luton Town 3-0 that day at Old Trafford, but the Boxing Day fixtures were and still are, very much looked forward to. Roy Cavanagh recalls Boxing Day 1967 when Wolverhampton Wanderers came to town. '*I loved the games around Christmas, my late father had taken me to the last Christmas Day game back in 1957 so the Boxing Day match was always a special one. When Wolves came, I was in my favourite position in the United Road Paddock with a few of my mates, particularly a former workmate called Ted Barry who I used to frequent the clubs around Salford and Manchester with. The crowd was a capacity 63,000 with an estimated 8,000 locked out. United were in great form winning 4-0 with Georgie getting a couple of the goals and playing like the superstar he now was.*

As Ted and I came out, the crush was all the way down United Road and then over the bridge where Hotel Football is now; Ted suddenly said 'my shoe has gone!' Fashion had even reached my mate Ted, and his new-fangled slip-on shoes were slipped off in the crush! It was seriously so tight I just said, 'Whatever you do don't try to bend down!'."

By the time the FA Cup started, unusually the last Saturday in January 1968 as opposed to the first, Manchester United were on a 13-match unbeaten run, clear at the top of the table and in the quarter-finals of the European Cup. The draw for the 3rd round was tough though, pairing United with a fine Tottenham Hotspur side, albeit at home. Tottenham had moved to a buying club with nine of the side all bought and even one of the other two, Joe Kinnear coming from St Albans as a 17-year old. Phil Beal was the other Tottenham player who had been a junior with the club. Manchester United had a much different approach, only three, Alex Stepney, Pat Crerand and Denis Law costing large fees, Tony Dune coming to United for a nominal fee from Shelbourne. The other seven, Burns, Sadler, Fitzpatrick, Best, Kidd, Charlton, and Aston were all products of the tremendous youth policy at Old Trafford.

The tie with Tottenham began a trilogy of matches over the next seven days: two cup ties and a league fixture between United and Spurs. The first cup tie was a superb match with Best and Charlton getting goals for United while newly signed Martin Chivers scored first and last on the day to send the 63,500 fans home content with witnessing a great game, but with no idea how the two sides could be separated. White Hart Lane would stage the replay and the league fixture, both games creating capacity 57,000 crowds. The cup tie went to extra-time before Jimmy Robertson scored the winner for Tottenham. This was a high-class Manchester United side though, and despite having to replace Denis Law after his knee problem flared again, they went to White Hart Lane three days later for the league match and won 2-1 with Best and Charlton repeating their scoring feats of the Saturday before.

Manchester City should have been the visitors to Old Trafford on 10 February 1968, but the Manchester weather won the day, and the game was called off. Still, on that Saturday night, the title was firmly Manchester United's to lose. One point clear of Leeds United but with two games in hand, six points clear of Manchester City on level games. They were out of the FA Cup, but with a squad of only 14 players who would have to play ten matches or more, and desperately wanting to win the European Cup, the FA Cup exit could have been a blessing in disguise.

A sign of the times, illustrating how footballers and fans had the chance to mingle on a Saturday night is recounted by Roy Cavanagh. Here he describes the last Saturday of February 1968. *United had gone to London to play Arsenal and won comfortably 2-0. Later that night I went to the Cabaret Club in Manchester which opened about 9.30pm. Just after 10, George Best strolled into the place, not mithered by anybody as he wandered over to sit with Malcolm Alison the Manchester City manager. Remember, George was then the most high profile footballer in Britain. Later this season he would be named the Football Writers Footballer of the Year, and also awarded the European Footballer of the Year trophy. Here he was walking, talking freely to who he wanted to, but despite being the poster boy of football then we did not have the 24-hour scrutiny, the 24 hour Sky Sports, the 24 hour Talk Sport, mobile phones in everybody's pockets or hands, it was truly a different world.'*

The following Wednesday, George and Manchester United were back into European Cup action with a visit from the Polish champions, Gornik Zabrze. They were from a mining, engineering and steel area and played with all the tenacity of such, particularly their goalkeeper Kostka who had a night to remember, even being applauded off the pitch at the end by the capacity crowd at Old Trafford. Luckily, he had been beaten twice, but from a corner count of 22-1 in United's favour, you can see the amount of work he had to endure! Two weeks later those two goals would become like gold dust when United visited Poland to play the second leg in Katowice, nearly 20 miles from Zabrze but having a stadium which would accommodate the anticipated 100,000 who wanted to see the match.

"Call this a newspaper, comrade?— There's no mention of England's team for the Fourth Test!"

Gornik were determined that the match should take place, arranging for 1,000 workers to clear the pitch and stadium. When Manchester United reached the stadium though, there seemed no way that the match could take place. A blizzard, on top of the snow already lying deep at the ground, meant there were serious concerns as to how the game could take place. A postponement though, was the last thing Matt Busby wanted and taking guidance from his staff and players it was felt, *'get the game on it is the same for both sides'*. One of those players was Pat Crerand, and in an interview with Roy Cavanagh, he discussed what Poland was like that night. *'The Poles are lovely people, but don't ask me to go there again! The food was terrible back in 1968, and the weather when we went there in March of that year was even worse! Matt was very wary of us playing that night with thick snow on top of a frozen pitch, but I said to him it was to our advantage, because on the goal lines there were six inches of snow which made the goals smaller, also we had that two-goal lead from the first leg, and there was no way that anyone could play football on a pitch like that which would make Gornik's job even harder.'*

With fires being lit in the ground by the capacity crowd, a seemingly constant noise from everybody there, by whatever means, the odds were stacked against United, but they battled marvellously, only conceding one second-half goal to Gornik's star player, inside-forward Lubanski. It was a very enjoyable journey home for all in the Manchester United party; their semi-final reward would take them to much warmer climes - Madrid to face the finest club in Europe, Real.

Whether it was a realisation that the chance of winning the European Cup was the priority this season, or whether it was the long list of injuries the team had suffered to key players like Denis Law, Nobby Stiles, Bill Foulkes and a still recovering David Herd, from a basically 14 player squad, maybe just simply bad luck, but the month of March 1968 was going to badly damage United's hopes of retaining the league title. They would lose three of the five league games played, including crucially one to their closest challenger, and local neighbour Manchester City.

One of those defeats was at Old Trafford against Chelsea on the Saturday after the Gornik home match. A packed-out Old Trafford just waited for their side to perform, but Chelsea were a very decent side. Chelsea itself was the epitome of the 'Swinging Sixties' a place loved by United's own George Best with its swagger, its show business clientele via Kings Road and home to its glamour. Well, they certainly brought all of that North and turned in a very fine display with their young centre forward Peter Osgood, the star man. He had suffered a bad leg break the season before, but this day he was outstanding as Chelsea deservedly won 3-1. There was an unkind song going around on the lines of 'Osgood was good is good no more' well anybody who saw his performance in this match knew they were seeing a very high-class footballer. When relegation-threatened Coventry City then beat United 2-0 days after the return from Poland, following the second leg of the European Cup tie, it did seem that the exertions of the efforts to win that trophy was taking precedence for the team. Reporting in the Guardian, David Lacey put it this way 'Manchester United's week in the snowy wastes of Silesia may well have cost them the league championship title.'

When Manchester City visited Old Trafford at the end of March, the position at the top of the league table saw Leeds United and Manchester United level on 45 points with Manchester having a game in hand but a slightly inferior goal difference, Manchester City and Liverpool being two points behind Manchester United. At the end of the match, City would be level! Another 62,000 plus crowd saw an early goal from George Best seemingly giving United advantage, but this City side, under the vibrant managership of Joe Mercer and Malcolm Alison had assembled a fine attacking side built around Francis Lee, Mike Summerbee and Colin Bell. All three displayed their skills to the full as they overturned George's goal and won, rather convincingly, 3-1. The month of March did end though with a morale-boosting victory away at Stoke City 4-2 with a young centre forward by the name of Alan Gowling given a goal scoring debut. He was a

19-year-old student studying at Manchester University and, therefore, still an amateur at the time of his debut. Such was his meteoric rise to the first team that Matt Busby had to request his absence from the Great Britain Olympic squad he was due to represent. He had, though, been very prominent in United's reserve side scoring over 20 goals at that time but with injuries again to Denis Law, and even to a returning David Herd from his broken leg, reinforcements were badly needed.

Another political assassination in America blighted the 1960s with the death of Martin Luther King in Memphis, Tennessee on the 4th April 1968. He was an American Baptist minister and activist who fought for civil rights in America from the mid-1950s, earning him the award of the Nobel Peace Prize in 1964. He had an inspiring rallying call to his followers of, 'I have a Dream'. A man whose memory is still strong 51 years on, even if his work is not complete...

Despite their loss of form, all was not yet lost in the league. The fixtures United played at the start, and end of April 1968, would provide what seemed the last chance to fight to retain the league title. Sadly, the two matches concerned, at home to Liverpool on 6 April and away at West Bromwich Albion on 29 April, would leave Manchester City firmly in the driving seat. The loss to Liverpool continued a depressing spell of United losing vital home fixtures following on from the defeats at home to Chelsea and Manchester City. This time the score was 2-1 despite another early George Best goal giving United the lead. The only positive thing to come out of this match was that with yet another full house of 63,000, Manchester United's average had exceeded the record held by Newcastle United of 56,473 for a season. Further capacity crowds would give Manchester United a then-record season average of 57,790.

A fifth young Manchester United player made his debut over Easter 1968, when reserve goalkeeper Jimmy Rimmer, an FA Youth Cup winner from 1964, replaced the injured Alex Stepney in the home match against Fulham. Jimmy had travelled as the goalkeeper substitute all over Europe this season covering 14,000 miles without getting a kick (or save in his case!) but was eased into first-team action with a welcome 3-0 home victory. That completed an Easter double over the London side which with a further victory over Sheffield United at home and a draw at Southampton gave renewed hope, putting United level at the top of the table with Manchester City, with just three matches to play.

Firstly though, there was the matter of a home European Cup semi-final against the legendary Real Madrid. Tickets for this match would have cost the capacity all-ticket crowd of 63,500 between 7/6 (37p) to stand to 40/- (£2) for the best seat. The receipts were £42,000, a British record for a single football match. Denis Law's injured knee was patched up for this vital game, and he led United to a fine 1-0 victory thanks to a George Best first-half goal. It was a season in which injuries threatened to derail United's ambitions. Bill Foulkes, Nobby Stiles and Denis Law would each miss over 20 matches in the league this season but were all patched up for the Madrid game as they desperately wanted to bring the European Cup to Manchester for Matt Busby and the memory of the Busby Babes ten years ago.

Despite their injury-ravaged squad and stuttering league form United still had a very real chance to retain their League title as they went into their last match in the month of April at West Bromwich Albion. This was a rearranged league match that should have taken place on Saturday 27 April 1968 but as West Bromwich Albion were playing, and winning, in the FA Cup semi-final that day against their local rivals Birmingham City, the match with United was moved to the Monday night. Incidentally, the other semi-final was played at Old Trafford with Everton taking on and beating Leeds United. With West Bromwich Albion winning their semi-final, one would have thought the advantage had shifted to Manchester United's favour as they would have been facing a side who possibly had been celebrating all weekend! A point for United would have put them in a dominant position. Clear at the top of the table over Manchester City with just two games left, both at home, against Newcastle United and Sunderland, while City had two seemingly difficult away matches at Tottenham Hotspur and Newcastle United to tackle.

However, in an amazing match at West Bromwich, the home side turned on the style and demolished United 6-3! Centre forward, Jeff Astle, was in great form scoring a hat-trick as David Sadler, deputising for the injured Bill Foulkes could not handle him. The result left City and United on level points, but City had the slender advantage of a better goal difference as the last two Saturday's of the season loomed.

On Saturday 4 May 1968, United returned to form as Old Trafford witnessed a majestic display by George Best against Newcastle United as he scored his first senior hat trick, which included two goals from the penalty spot in a resounding 6-0 victory. The timing of this display was perfect as George was announced as the Footballer of the Year by the Footballer Writers Association that weekend, becoming the youngest recipient of the award and also the third Manchester United to be so awarded, following Johnny Carey and Bobby Charlton. Despite the emphatic display, the sour note of the day for United followers was the news of City's 3-1 victory at Tottenham which meant they went into the last day as leaders.

In a moment eerily similar to what would happen some 44 years further on, Manchester United played Sunderland on the last day of the season needing to not only win but also hope that Manchester City would not win their match at Newcastle. This time though, unlike what would happen in 2012, the title was decided on points and not goal difference as City won a thrilling match 4-3 in the North East, while United were surprisingly defeated 2-1 at home by Sunderland. The position of runners up, following the championship of the previous season showed the consistency of Manchester United. Injuries together with the competing interest of the European Cup had proven too much in the League. The season was far from over though, and the possibility remained that they could eclipse it all by winning their European Cup semi-final the following Wednesday in the cauldron of the Bernabeu Stadium in Madrid.

Pos	Club	Pld	W	D	L	GF	GA	Pts
1	Manchester City	42	26	6	10	86	43	58
2	Manchester United	42	24	8	10	89	55	56
3	Liverpool	42	22	11	9	71	40	55

While David Sadler had come under scrutiny playing as centre-half after being on the end of a very physical performance from Jeff Astle a couple of weeks earlier; he showed his worth and versatility by slotting into the number ten shirt as a replacement for the unfit Denis Law in Madrid. David had made his Manchester United debut as a centre-forward back in 1963 as a 17-year-old, and here he was five years on, appearing in a number ten shirt following his many fine appearances as a centre-half and left-half. Matt Busby also brought Shay Brennan back for the second-leg as a replacement for Francis Burns who had appeared in most of the European Cup ties and could count himself unlucky to be missing out as the final stages approached. A crowd of 120,000 awaited in the Spanish capital, with the vast majority expecting yet another European Cup Final appearance for their favourites. Or would, finally at their fourth attempt, Manchester United fulfil their destiny?

Playing a more defensive 4-3-3 formation, Manchester United slotted Sadler alongside Crerand and Charlton in midfield with Best and Aston wide of Kidd, with defensively, Brennan, Foulkes, Stiles and Dunne protecting Stepney in goal. Formations though went out of the window by half time as Madrid strolled, contemptuously it seemed, into a 3-1 lead. In the subdued dressing room, Matt Busby calmly informed his team that because of the one-goal lead from Old Trafford, they were only one goal behind Madrid, not two. The message certainly seemed to have got through, and as Sadler moved forward more, it was he who got on the end of a Best header to score a vital second goal. 3-3 on aggregate and a Madrid side and crowd, suddenly realising the dangers they were in. George Best again rose to the occasion and sublimely ghosted past two Madrid players before pulling the ball back invitingly to an onrushing forward. Remarkably, it was not a forward though, but the unlikely presence of centre-half Bill Foulkes who guided the ball home to equalise on the night, and more importantly, put Manchester United 4-3 up on aggregate. It was a very poignant moment as Bill had played in Manchester United's very first European Cup match back in September 1956.

THE HOLY GRAIL.
EUROPEAN CUP FINAL WEDNESDAY 29 MAY 1968 WEMBLEY MANCHESTER UNITED V BENFICA.

That Manchester United lined up at Wembley on 29 May 1968 with the opportunity of winning the European Cup, Matt Busby's long-cherished holy grail provides an astonishing testament to the great man. He had defied the Football League back in 1956 when first entering the competition. No doubt at the time he believed he was building an exceptional team that would go on to win the competition. To have the fortitude and acumen to build a new team just ten years after the Busby Babes had been decimated when returning from playing a match in the same competition is simply remarkable. Memories from the past, many too painful to bear, were everywhere that unforgettable night. Worryingly for United, star man, Denis Law was lying in hospital recovering from injury as the final was played. If their destiny were to be fulfilled, they would have to do it without the King. Despite this, one particular memory provided hope for the team. Two years previously Manchester United had produced one of their greatest ever performances when they had beaten Benfica in their own Lisbon fortress; now they were just 90 minutes away from winning the European Cup in their national stadium. In fact, 120 minutes was needed, as the match would eventually go into extra time, as Benfica scored a late equaliser to United's opening goal, a rare header from Bobby Charlton. In the first 15-minute half of extra time, George Best moved onto a long clearance and moved effortlessly into the Benfica area, gliding past their goalkeeper before rolling the ball into an empty net. Birthday boy 19-year-old Brian Kidd scored United's third and, fittingly, the match was sealed with a lovely second goal of the night from Bobby Charlton. Finally, all of Manchester United's supporters the world over could believe that their club, Manchester United, were Champions of Europe! The Man of the Match was outside left John Aston, son of a former United great of the same name who had helped win the FA Cup of 1948 and the league title of 1952. The present John Aston had to live in the shadow of George Best, Bobby Charlton, and Denis Law but came to his own this night as he destroyed the Benfica right back and facilitated many an attack down the left flank. He had been instrumental in United reaching the final setting up vital goals against both Sarajevo and Real Madrid in the Old Trafford ties and this night truly became a top player in his own right. Sadly, the fate of life and the game of football would see another side of the coin for John three months on when he broke his leg in an early-season match at

Manchester City.

It is hard for the authors to put into words the events and emotions of that night, and so in a different slant to this match which is etched into Manchester United folklore, we have memories from some of the leading people on that day via their interviews with Roy Cavanagh 36 years ago. They are Matt Busby the manager, George Best a goal scorer, Alex Stepney who made a vital save at 1-1, Pat Crerand who helped dominate midfield, and Martin Edwards, son of the Manchester United chairman that night.

These are their interviews with Roy;

SIR MATT BUSBY

'I'm going to see the boss and tell him exactly what I think' Those words had been heard many, many times over the years in the Old Trafford dressing room as one player expressed a grievance to another and promptly marched up the stairs to see Matt Busby.

Ten or 15 minutes later, as the player closed the door quietly behind him on the way out, the same phrase has also very often been heard. *'Thanks boss, I'm sorry to have troubled you and thanks again for dropping me/ refusing to give me a rise/ or placing me on the transfer list, oh! And thanks for being so understanding.'*

There was absolutely no doubt about it; Matt Busby was THE boss of Manchester United. Meeting him in his old office was one of the most memorable days of my life. Obviously, the European Cup win of 1968 came up, and I asked him what he remembered about the goal that settled the issue, early in extra time.

'George went off on one of his runs after he had gathered a long kick upfield from Alex Stepney. As usual with George, he kept me in suspense until the last possible moment, before he slid the ball home. It reminded me in many ways of Billy Whelan's marvellous goal in Bilbao in 1957. When the final whistle went, winning the trophy was wonderful for me, and also the club and our supporters, I felt we had achieved my life's ambitions.'

GEORGE BEST

Back in 1983, I co-wrote a book with the popular ex-footballer now pundit, Fred Eyre. One afternoon he rang to ask if I wanted to go and interview George Best over in Rawtenstall where he was doing an after-dinner talk. Rawtenstall had never seemed so good! Here is what the match-winner had to say.

'I don't think the Benfica defenders had forgotten the last time we had met a couple of years earlier and most of the match they gave me very little room to play. My eyes lit up, though when Alex's massive kick landed just right for me to waltz into the area and pick my spot. That should have been the start of the next great Manchester United era, our domination of European football, as it turned out it was the end of the club's dream. Manchester United had climbed the mountain, and it now appeared to be content to

slither down the other side.'

George was speaking seriously but passionately now.

'It's always difficult to replace faithful and good players who have served the club well, but I thought Manchester United needed to be ruthless… and they weren't, so players who needed replacing were allowed to play on, and the team slowly began to slide.'

He summed up by saying, *'My first five years as a Manchester United player were unbelievable, and the rest should have been.'*

A deeper thinker about the game of football than a lot of people gave him credit for, George Best is still the greatest footballer I have seen…

ALEX STEPNEY;

Imagine leaving the East End of London for the West End, then being sent to Manchester and winning the League Title and European Cup within two years of being there! Alex Stepney did not just do all this; he made it happen with a memorable save in the last ten minutes of the European Cup Final. This is what it was like to be at the centre of the action.

'I had little to do for most of the match when Benfica suddenly cut through our defence to equalise. In what seemed their next attack, it was a straight challenge with Eusebio and me. He was a superb player, but he had a tendency to be a glory hunter. He really should have lobbed me; instead, he tried to blast the net off, and luckily, the ball stayed in my grasp.'

That save by Alex most definitely won the European Cup for Manchester United. The final whistle went soon after giving the chance of 30 minutes extra time, which resulted in the famous 4-1 victory. It was the highlight of Alex's career, although he quickly praised the man who was responsible for it all.

'Matt Busby was the driving force all the Manchester United players had in their efforts to win the European Cup. I owe him everything in football. His whole manner made you want to win it for him. He was like a favourite Grandfather really…'

PAT CRERAND;

Having left Glasgow Celtic in 1963 to join Manchester United, the 1968 European Cup Final gave Pat a great chance to join his former team as winners of the famous trophy following their victory over Inter Milan the previous season. He recalled the after match events just as much though!

'Winning the match, deservedly so in extra-time sealed a night of great tension which affected everyone, winning was everything to us. Straight after though both Bobby Charlton and myself were so physically exhausted that we could not even join in the after-match celebrations. I felt ill, really ill. Then I was physically sick, and Jack Crompton was very good to Bobby and me and arranged a taxi back to our hotel. I can remember crawling into bed and the next thing it was the following morning! The only medical explanation was a nervous reaction to the strain of the final.'

MARTIN EDWARDS;

If you were young, handsome, wealthy AND chairman of Manchester United, it must seem like Christmas every day of the week! That was my thought when I met Martin in 1983, three years after he had become the top man at United following the death of his father, Louis. While it was Louis who had been chairman of the club on that memorable night at Wembley Stadium in 1968, Martin recalled his feelings of the night.

'When we reached the final in 1968, nothing could stop me from attending. I was not a director at the time, but I did get a good seat! During the first half Benfica seemed determined not to suffer their same fate as in Lisbon two years earlier and played a defensive game, which in fairness was foreign to them. When Bobby Charlton scored with a header, it seemed certain to be our day. Their late equaliser changed matters, and it took a great save from Alex Stepney to keep us in the match. Indeed, waiting for extra time to start was probably the worst part of the game as Benfica had come good in those last ten minutes. Thankfully, George did his stuff, young Brian Kidd scored a birthday goal, and Bobby joyously thumped home the fourth. That was it, 4-1 Champions of Europe!'

Finally, one last memory that illustrates better than words could do, the joy that the European Cup triumph brought to the people of Manchester. Co-author Carl Abbott recalls a boyhood memory that he will never forget. *'Stepney, Brennan, Dunne, Crerand, Foulkes, Stiles, Best, Kidd, Charlton, Sadler, Aston. That is the line-up of the team that won the European Cup in 1968. I was 5-years-old at the time, and one of my earliest memories is my dad seemingly jumping through the ceiling after a United goal. The final is forever etched on my mind courtesy of a print of a cartoon by the Guardian cartoonist Papas that took pride of place on the wall of my childhood home. The cartoon was presented by Papas to the directors of the Manchester Evening News, where my grandad was a printer. He was at the final that night and had managed to get one of the limited number of prints that were produced. As a boy, I would gaze at this print, looking at all the marvellous details of the celebrations in Manchester. The team is listed courtesy of a scroll held aloft by an angel, and I can't imagine the number of times I read that list. I hope that the copy of the print gives the readers a fraction of the joy that I have had over all the years that I have gazed at it.'*

A week after the euphoria of such an emotional victory, politics took centre stage in the world with the assassination of Robert F. Kennedy, the brother of John F. Kennedy who had suffered the same fate five years earlier. Robert was preparing to follow his brother by standing for the American Presidency when he was shot in California. Back in Britain, Prime Minister Harold Wilson had yet another part to play in the link between football and politics. Indeed, Harold Wilson was famous for a quote of the time which was, 'A week is a long time in politics', well it certainly was in life so soon after the Wembley victory, as Harold Wilson bestowed a Knighthood on Alexander Matthew Busby. Roy Cavanagh would meet Matt Busby in the early 1980s, indeed do a 25-minute interview with him around the time they were both on Willie Morgan's testimonial committee. Here is what Roy recalls of those times.

'Matt Busby immediately came over as a favourite uncle or grandad. He had a strong Scottish brogue, and you could not help but think of what enormous strength he must have had, in various ways. Physically after receiving the last rites a couple of times while in the Munich hospital after the air crash in 1958. Mentally as he combined the requirement of winning matches and trophies, with dealing with player needs and the difficult decisions of picking teams and letting players leave.

He had been born into a coal mining family in Belshill, an area which incredibly would also produce Jock Stein and Bill Shankly, two other managerial giants of the era Matt Busby presided over. Matt had lost his father to a sniper in the First World War so soon had responsibility thrust on him. Football rather than mining was going to be Matt's outlet in life, and he came south when 18 to join Manchester City. At City, he was converted from an inside right to right half and in the 1930s would play in two successive FA Cup Finals for them. In 1933 it was a losing medal against a Dixie Dean led Everton before in 1934 it was Matt Busby walking up those Wembley steps to receive a winner's medal against Portsmouth.

After Manchester City, it would be Liverpool where Matt Busby found fame, ironic that two of the biggest of all Manchester United rivals would be club's he would play for. Indeed, Liverpool were keen to make him their manager, but the Second World War had changed many people, and Matt had been approached by Louis Rocca, a man himself whose legend is linked in Manchester United's history, to become the new leader of Old Trafford when hostilities ended.

At the age of 36, Matt Busby commenced a managerial career which would lead him to be the greatest manager English football had ever seen since the legendary Herbert Chapman with both Huddersfield Town and Arsenal in the 1920s and 1930s. The FA Cup triumphs of 1948 and 1963, league titles in 1952, 1956, 1957, 1965 and 1967 put Matt Busby on the highest level, his strength showing through yet again as he led Manchester United into European football against the wishes of the football authorities to glory in 1968. To be sat opposite Matt Busby, one to one, just over a coffee, was one of the greatest moments of my life. He was a true gentleman, a true hero; he was Mr Manchester United.'

Chapter Eleven

ESTUDIANTES!

1968-69

From their peak on 29 May 1968 as Champions of Europe, Manchester United would by 17 August 1974, be a Second Division club. They would also then be under the third manager burdened with the task of replacing the legendary Sir Matt Busby. This startling descent started with the 1968-69 season despite the potential of the season lifting the club to new heights as they competed in the challenge match for the title of World Club Champions against the Argentine side Estudiantes. It begs the question was the reaching the 'Holy Grail', the moment Manchester United took their foot off the pedal and started their decline? If you consider George Best's thoughts in the previous chapter that after that European Cup triumph United just did not invest enough on players to replace those who were beginning to reach the end of their career, it is difficult to argue otherwise. For the senior players around George the triumph in the European Cup marked the end of a long journey, George was at an age when there still should have been many more triumphs on his glorious journey – sadly as we know, it was not to be.

Certainly, the 1968-69 season would see a nosedive in the level of performance in the league that was unacceptable after the quality of performances of the previous five seasons. Progress in the FA Cup and the attempt to retain the European Cup did at least provide some measure of success, while the World Club challenge propelled Manchester United into the highest level a club could compete.

There was little thought of decline on the first day of the new season when the return of a fit Denis Law provided a big boost to the European Cup holders as they entertained Everton before a packed Old Trafford crowd, who witnessed a deserved 2-1 victory. The return of the King, a truly world-class forward, was especially important as the forward line lacked strength in depth now as David Herd had left United to join Stoke City after seven excellent years as a very fine centre-forward. David was underrated for a lot of his time at Old Trafford, but not by anybody who knew their football. He was a regular goalscorer, a very fine team player, and a vital part of some of Manchester United's finest forward lines as they won two league titles, the FA Cup and of course the European Cup in the 1960s.

The day after the Everton match, a part of British history disappeared as the last passenger steam train ran from Liverpool to Carlisle and back. The last train was called 'The Fifteen Guinea Special'. Since 1968 steam trains are still regularly seen on heritage excursions, but no longer part of mainline services.

During the following week, Manchester United had worrying news straight after the West Bromwich Albion match on the Wednesday night. United lost the game 3-1, but more worrying than the result was the fact that Denis Law had suffered more knee pain during the match. Over the past 12 months, Denis had undergone a previous unsuccessful knee operation after which he had tried comebacks, and he had been assured that his latest knee operation had been a complete success. Thankfully, this time, it was not too serious, and he soon returned to the side.

He was to miss, however, the Manchester derby at Maine Road as the European Champions United met their near-neighbours City, who were the current league champions. The 63,000 crowd surprisingly did not see any goals but, sadly, they did see the disastrous leg break suffered by winger John Aston, the man who had been the 'Man of the Match' in the European Cup Final only three months previously. The crowd also saw the harder side of Sir Matt Busby who was, obviously, very disappointed after suffering a second heavy defeat to West Bromwich Albion inside three months. Busby reacted by omitting Shay Brennan and Pat Crerand, which with injuries to Bill Foulkes and Denis Law, meant a host of chances to the younger players, Frank Kopel, John Fitzpatrick and Jimmy Ryan, while the still young Francis Burns also returned.

These changes did not last long though, as Chelsea came to Old Trafford and hammered Manchester United 4-0, a result that immediately sent Sir Matt Busby into the transfer market with the signing of Burnley winger Willie Morgan for a then British record fee of over £100,000. Willie was also a Scottish international, and being young himself, obviously modelling himself on his new teammate George Best with his style on and off the football pitch. He was also handed the number seven shirt with George switching over to the left-wing, number 11.

A troubling political situation for Europe occurred over 20 - 21 August with a Russian led invasion of Czechoslovakia in brutal response to Political Liberalisation. The turmoil was also to have a major effect on European football competitions as countries within the Iron Curtain close to Czechoslovakia such as Bulgaria, Hungary and Poland all withdrew their teams from European involvement. This, of course, reduced the number of teams to an uneven number resulting in some sides getting byes to the later rounds.

From Manchester United's point of view, while the World Club Challenge was looming against Estudiantes, they also had their European Cup to defend. Having a fully fit Denis Law was going to be vital if they were able to cope with these pressures and he certainly showed everybody how much he wanted to be involved as Waterford from Ireland provided the first challenge. Denis scored a first-leg hat-trick in a 3-1 victory over in Dublin, following it up with four goals in the second leg as United won 7-0, 10-1 on aggregate. Seven goals in two games, the King was back!

While we were firmly in the football season, the cricket world was rocked on 17 September 1968 when South Africa refused to allow Basil D'Oliveira's inclusion in the MCC touring party because of their segregation and apartheid policy. Basil was a fine player of South African Cape Coloured background who had gained English citizenship in 1964. A fine cricketer, he had been left out of the original touring party, in what many felt was an unnecessary bow down to South Africa, but he was now called up due to an injury. The decision of South Africa to not allow him to enter and play tests for the MCC caused South Africa to be ostracised, and it would be 22 years before they played test matches again.

For Manchester United there now followed the huge challenge of playing the Champions of South America, Estudiantes of Argentina. The United team and official party left Manchester on Saturday 21 September 1968 straight after their 3-1 home victory over Newcastle United and travelled to South America via Paris, Madrid and Rio de Janeiro. Willie Morgan, new to life at Manchester United, recalled the two legs in conversation with Roy Cavanagh. *These were my first big club games. At Burnley, we had been in the Inter-Cities Fairs Cup, but this was way above anything I'd known. Argentina was nice, lovely hotel, lots of golf, but when we arrived it was an incredible sight at the Buenos Aires airport, with literally hundreds of reporters and photographers all wanting "El Assassin", "Where's Stiles?" they shouted. They would not believe this inoffensive bloke with glasses was Nobby! They were out to crucify him, and of course, they got their way during the match when he was sent off for just raising his hands at an offside decision. We were truly robbed in both legs of this match. Bill Foulkes had a perfectly good goal disallowed, and despite us losing 1-0 we were grateful to get away without serious injury, and really fancied our chances at Old Trafford of becoming the first British winners of this trophy'.*

Glasgow Celtic had been the first British club to play for this trophy the previous season when they had played Racing Club of Buenos Aires, winning 1-0 in Glasgow, losing 2-1 in Argentina and then playing in a truly brutal third tie in Montevideo, the capital of Uruguay. Six players, four from Celtic, two from Racing Club were sent off, and it was Racing Club who won 1-0 and took the trophy. Indeed, many people thought that Manchester United should not compete because of what had happened 12 months previously, but of course, Sir Matt Busby was not the type to allow outside issues to take centre stage. Incidentally, because of the time difference, the only way to hear about the match in Argentina when United visited was via a crackly radio in the early hours of the morning over here!

The acrimony of the match was reflected in the press reports of the

'Sickening travesty of football'

time. Writing in the Daily Mirror Frank McGhee claimed that *'Estudiantes were set on treachery, provocation and violence'*. Hugh McIlvaney in The Guardian described the match as a *'Sickening travesty of football'*. His match report is excoriating in its criticism of the Argentinian side and their methods: *'Manchester United went to Argentina, hoping, if scarcely believing, that the belated but forceful intervention of FIFA in the organisation of the Inter-Continental Cup, the so-called World Club Championship of football, would cleanse the competition of, the rancour and brutality that have characterised it since its inception in 1960. They left with further proof that Argentine footballers can hardly be relied upon to observe the Geneva Convention, let alone the basic principles of sportsmanship.'* In what by today's standards seems a shocking statement he went on to say that the match was: *'another painful indication that football when it involves a clash of races tends, like so much of international sport, to be perverted to a point where it amounts to an exercise in degradation: of players, of officials, of spectators and everyone else connected with it.'* Shocking as though that statement may be, it gives an idea of the rarity of such encounters at the time and the huge mistrust and animosity between the sides. That said, there is no doubt that United's treatment in Argentina was beyond the pale. Sir Stanley Rous, President of FIFA, stating that *'the outstanding feature of the match was the quite remarkable tolerance of the United players.'*

Against this background, there was never any doubt that Old Trafford would have a sell-out 63,500 all ticket crowd for the second-leg, a season highest with tickets costing from 10/- (50p) groundside (standing) to 60/- (£3) for a cantilever centre stand seat. The fans were to be disappointed though as Willie Morgan recalls: *'Before the game, a few of the team were carrying knocks which meant the team was not selected until the day of the match. It did not get better when we kicked off as Estudiantes scored early on from their left winger nicknamed 'The Witch'. Veron was his real name, but I must admit we called him a few nicknames when he scored! (A note here, Veron's son, Juan Sebastian, would in later years become a world-famous footballer, even signing for Manchester*

United in 2001). Now 2-0 up on aggregate, Estudiantes were not for losing that advantage and used every trick in the book (and outside it) they kicked, spat, and generally stopped you at every opportunity. Denis Law received a savage kick on the shin which forced him off whilst both George and myself were given a right going over, George turning around and thumping one of their players which saw them both sent off. We got a free-kick from that as it was retaliation from George, from it Pat Crerand floated the ball over for me to knock into the net. 1-1 on the night but we still needed another goal to take it to a third match. Incredibly, with the last kick, Brian Kidd did get the ball into the net, but the referee had blown for full time as the ball went in. To say the least a very sad end'.

The match had soured relations between the FAs of England and Argentina to breaking point. Estudiantes had been scheduled to play friendlies against Birmingham City and Arsenal following on from the clash with United. In the event, they went straight home after playing Inter Milan in Italy. The papers reported the rumour that the Argentine FA had ordered them home.

A reminder that life goes on outside the acrimony in the world of football at the time was provided by news that the space programme was moving forward with the thought even of having the first man on the moon mooted by both America and Russia. A major step forward for this came about on 11 October 1968 when America's three-man mission, Apollo 7, orbited the Moon. Russia had had many attempts via their Soyuz craft and the race to have somebody land on the Moon was not now so fanciful...

With their World Club attempt over, Manchester United got back to league action, but from that victory over Newcastle United on 21 September until 18 January 1969, a total of 15 league matches, only three were won, one away at the bottom side Queens Park Rangers, one at home to then league leaders Liverpool and the other at home to Wolverhampton Wanderers. A combination of injuries to key players and a possible loss of desire certainly had Manchester United in an unfamiliar mid-table position. They were, of course, the team everybody wanted to beat as European Cup holders, but there were now serious requirements to strengthen, with positions at right-back, centre-half, midfield to fill and another striker needed (sounds familiar in 2019!) whilst Sir Matt Busby's drive and determination to shape the future was in question after surely he had fulfilled all his ambitions?

During the poor run, youngsters such as Carlo Sartori as a substitute at Tottenham Hotspur, then alongside Steve James for their full debuts away at Liverpool, appeared. Decent players as they were, perhaps the production line from the juniors had also reached its limits. In fairness, the injury crisis was severe, with Dunne, Burns, Foulkes, Sadler, Morgan, Law, Kidd and Best all missing at Liverpool. Most were back for the match against Leeds United at Old Trafford on 2 November 1968 which was a meeting between the holders of the European Cup in Manchester United and the Inter-Cities Fairs Cup in Leeds United who had won that trophy in a final carried over to this season against Hungarian side Ferencvaros. A hard-fought goalless draw ensued at Old Trafford between the two European titleholders.

A real European night returned to Old Trafford with a tie against Belgian champions RSC Anderlecht, the side Manchester United had played their first-ever European tie back in September 1956. Because of the withdrawal of the Czechoslovakian, Bulgarian, Hungarian and Polish champions, the European Cup had an unbalanced number of sides, 14, at this stage of the competition, so AC Milan and Benfica had the advantage of drawing byes into the quarter-final stage.

A crowd of 51,000 turned up to see if United could turn their distinctly average league form into the European Cup holders they were. Losing both wingers, Willie Morgan and George Best beforehand did not raise confidence but an outstanding performance from Denis Law with two goals, his ninth in three European ties, helped secure a comfortable 3-0 victory in the first leg. Oh, how they needed that comfort zone as they hung on for an aggregate victory thanks to an early goal from Italian born Carlo Sartori whose family had come over to Manchester when he was very young. His goal in Brussels proved priceless as the Belgian side scored three themselves to win 3-1 on the night, United going through 4-3 on aggregate to the quarter-finals.

The European and the FA Cups looked the only chance of success as Christmas 1968 approached, with United having gained only 20 points from their first 21 matches, 15 points behind the then leaders Liverpool. That this inconsistent league form would be reversed when United beat Liverpool 1-0 thanks to a Denis Law goal at Old Trafford, was welcome but very frustrating for the 60,000 crowd.

As 1969 arrived, America elected Richard Nixon as their 37th President, starting a reign which would certainly go down in history. He would be President when the Vietnam War was ended, see America land a man on the moon, end the military draft, ease relations with both China and Russia and yet end up resigning before almost certain impeachment under what became known as the Watergate scandal.

For Manchester United, 1969 began with a visit to Devon to play Fourth Division Exeter City in the FA Cup, with a 3-1 victory ensuring progress to the 4th round of the FA Cup and a home tie against high flying Third Division side Watford. In the days leading up to the match, however, there came the sensational news that Sir Matt Busby was retiring as manager of Manchester United at the end of the season, when he would become the club's General Manager, leaving a new person to take control of the side. No social media of course in those days, meaning snippets in the press were the only news of who that might be.

I FEEL SORRY FOR MAN WHO TAKES ON MATT'S MANTLE

The press were fulsome in their praise of Sir Matt, both as a manager and as a man. In the Guardian Eric Todd detailed the managerial record of this *'most philosophical of footballers'* going on to say: *'In support, if support be necessary, of Sir Matt's philosophy, his persuasive powers, and his remarkable influence on his men, one has only to consider United honours list since he took command. It makes formidable reading,: European Champion Clubs' Cup Winners once; First Division Champions five times, and runners-up six times; European Cup Winners' Cup quarter-finalists; FA Challenge Cup winners twice and beaten finalists twice; European Cup semi-finalists three times; FA Charity Shield winners three times, joint holders twice, beaten finalists three times; FA Youth Cup winners six times; Fairs' Cup semi-finalists once; Central League winners three times. And many trophies in minor competitions.'* In the same paper, Hugh McIlvanney focussed on the man with the memorable statement that *'behind the irresistibly courteous front, the infallible memory for faces, there is a real and lovable man, perhaps the biggest British football has produced.'* There is little time for sentiment in football, though. Reporting on the press conference at which the news that Sir Matt would be stepping down, Frank McGee was already looking to the future. Prophetically he headlined his report *'I feel sorry for the man who takes on Matt's mantle.'*

A huge Old Trafford crowd of 63,498 serenaded Sir Matt at the Watford game, but it was the Third Division side who celebrated by gaining a 1-1 draw to take United to Vicarage Road for a lucrative replay.

Denis Law was back in fine goalscoring form, scoring United's goal in the 1-1 draw and then scoring both goals as United won the replay 2-0. We have reflected a lot on Denis Law in this book, now in 1969 as the decade was coming to a close, his goalscoring and general football awareness need praising again. He particularly loved the FA Cup competition, and in all, he would score 34 goals in the FA Cup alone in his Manchester United career. Despite his crippling knee problems over the past 12 months, after the Watford replay, he had still scored 24 goals in 27 matches across all competitions this season. Denis Law is, without doubt, one of Manchester United's all-time greats.

Progress in the FA Cup meant fixture congestion with three games in the two cup competitions Manchester United were involved in occurring in the same week. The three matches attracted 188,516 spectators to Old Trafford and as Roy Cavanagh recalls. *'Having to rearrange a fifth-round replay against Birmingham City at Old Trafford as the sixth-round was due on the following Saturday and play the already arranged home quarter-final tie in the European Cup against Rapid Vienna, meant it was an expensive time to be a supporter! Denis Law continued his incredible form by scoring a hat-trick on the Monday night against Second Division Birmingham City as United started the week off in great style with a 6-2 replay victory in front of 62,000 at Old Trafford. Jimmy Greenhoff played for Birmingham that night, ten years on he would score a memorable semi-final replay goal for Manchester United against Liverpool to take them to the 1979 FA Cup Final.*

Having beaten Birmingham, it meant a scramble to get tickets for the following Saturday's quarter-final against Everton, while also attending the European Cup tie against Rapid Vienna. Rapid deserved a lot of respect as they had knocked Real Madrid out in the previous round. This time it was not Denis Law carrying United but a dazzling display by George Best who scored twice, with a goal from Willie Morgan, getting his first European Cup action, helping United forget their unconvincing league form as they cruised home 3-0 before 63,118 fans.

That number increased to 63,464 for the visit of Everton in the Sixth Round of the FA Cup on Saturday. Sadly, defensively Everton were far superior to Birmingham and Rapid Vienna, and as the game looked to be heading for a replay, Joe Royle scored the winner to knock United out of the FA Cup.'

This defeat seemed to knock Manchester United's performances even further in the league, as they went on a three-match scoreless run, four as they drew 0-0 in Vienna in the second leg with Rapid, although that, of course, meant yet another European Cup semi-final. The goal drought was finally broken, albeit in a 3-2 defeat at Chelsea, but then exploded in an incredible match at Old Trafford against bottom of the table Queens Park Rangers. They had achieved promotion to the First Division for the first time in their history and were visiting Old Trafford for the first time. They went away with an 8-1 defeat, Manchester United's highest league score since football returned after the Second World War. Willie Morgan marked the occasion to score his first-ever hat-trick, with George Best (2), Nobby Stiles, Brian Kidd and a goal from the returning John Aston completing the rout. A certain Rodney Marsh was the sole Rangers goal scorer.

This result looked to be a turning point and preceded Manchester United's longest unbeaten run of the whole season of seven matches, running from this match up to their 3-1 victory over Nottingham Forest. Ironically (or was it?!) the day after the unbeaten run was broken by a 2-1 defeat at Coventry City, the successor to Sir Matt Busby was announced by chairman Louis C. Edwards. It was to many, a surprise name, former Busby Babe and now reserve team coach, Wilf McGuinness. Even in those days, well before social media was everywhere, names had been bandied about as to who would succeed Sir Matt Busby. The man who seemed to be the favourite was Jock Stein, the Glasgow Celtic manager who amongst his many triumphs had been to become the first manager in Britain to win the European Cup 12 months before Sir Matt. Jock Stein and Liverpool's manager Bill Shankly, along with Sir Matt Busby all came from the same area of Scotland, mining places around Glasgow. They became the greatest managers of their time, and on reflection, as good as any of all-time. Sir Matt the seemingly friendly grandfather type, who had so much strength it was incredible to comprehend, Bill Shankly, looking you unnervingly straight in the eye, a believer, a man people followed, and Jock Stein in many ways, a combination of the two. There was no doubt detailed discussion on him coming to Old Trafford, but he finally decided to stay in Glasgow and United looked elsewhere.

Wilf McGuinness was the choice, a former England and Manchester schoolboy captain, understudy to the legendary Duncan Edwards, then the Manchester United number six until a broken leg in 1959 virtually ended his playing career, although not before he had made two appearances for England. As a coach, he soon made an impression at Old Trafford coaching young players then having a very successful time as the reserve team coach alongside the legendary Jimmy Murphy. An attempt to rekindle his playing career, sadly failed but Wilf continued as a very successful coach, soon also catching the eye of Alf Ramsey as England youth coach and then being elevated to the backroom staff as Alf, then to become Sir Alf Ramsey, led England to their glorious success in the 1966 World Cup. He would, however, have very close links to quite a few younger players at Old Trafford who had moved from his reserve side to the first team such as Brain Kidd, Francis Burns, Frank Kopel, John Fitzpatrick, Steve James, Carlo Sartori, Alan Gowling and Jimmy Rimmer. Of course, coaching and managing are two very different roles, and Wilf would soon have to replace his close personal friendships with such as Bobby Charlton, Nobby Stiles and Shay Brennan, and become their 'Boss'.

On the same day as Wilf McGuinness was announced, not as manager of Manchester United, but their chief coach, the first test flight of Concorde 002, was taken under the guidance of Brian Trubshaw, weeks after he had done similar with Concorde 001 the identical French prototype. The football world now waited to see how Wilf McGuinness would fly as the guide of Manchester United…

One of those reserves Wilf McGuinness had nurtured was goalkeeper Jimmy Rimmer, who had travelled across Europe the past two seasons as Alex Stepney's understudy but had just been given a real chance to become Manchester United's number one while Sir Matt Busby was still the number one as Manchester United manager. Despite the goalkeeping change, United suffered a couple of away defeats before beating Burnley at Old

Trafford 2-0. The game was significant for the presentation of the European Footballer of the Year award to George Best, which made it an incredible hat trick for Manchester United. They became the first, and still only, European club to have three separate players in the same side, Denis Law, Bobby Charlton and now George Best awarded this prestigious honour.

These three European winners had the opportunity to show their pedigree as the first leg of the European Cup semi-final arrived with a visit to the San Siro Stadium in Milan to play AC. A big difference for Manchester United supporters was that they could see the action 'live' as, like the experiment two years earlier at the Arsenal away league match, the game from Italy was transmitted back to Manchester via closed-circuit TV to giant screens on the Old Trafford pitch. Sadly, the viewing from Italy did not make good watching as a fine Milan side won 2-0, United not helped by a John Fitzpatrick sending off.

There was a long three-week gap between the two legs as, in theory, the league season ended on the Saturday after the first-leg, but United's last match against Leicester City was put back until after the Second Leg, Leicester losing the FA Cup Final in between 1-0 against Manchester City.

AC Milan arrived at Old Trafford for a Thursday night match, with the Old Trafford stadium packed out with 63,000 fans, conscious that Manchester United's whole season lay on this tie. Their cup runs in both the FA and European Cups had masked a very disappointing league season, which Manchester United would eventually finish in 11th place. While United had their own world-class players in Charlton, Law and Best, AC Milan carried class players themselves in 1966 German World Cup finalist Karl Schnellinger, 1958 Swedish World Cup finalist in Kurt Hamrin and Italian star internationals Giovanni Trapattoni and Gianni Rivera.

An incredible atmosphere saw a tight match, which a Bobby Charlton goal for United, only helped intensify. When Denis Law was sure, as were the 63,000 present, that he had equalised at the Stretford End, they cascaded down in huge swaying motions, the noise from the crowd seeming to threaten the roof on that stand to come off. Sadly, the French referee did not think the ball had crossed the line which infuriated the entire crowd. During the second-half, the Milan goalkeeper Fabio Cudicini (father of future Chelsea goalkeeper Carlo) suggested he had been hit by various things thrown at him by the Stretford End crowd. This slowed the game down while he received prolonged treatment, and it was AC Milan who celebrated at the final whistle as they would be going to Madrid for the final two weeks later. There they would beat an emerging Dutch side, Ajax Amsterdam 4-1, if only that 'goal' of Denis Law had been allowed Manchester United would have had the chance of at least a third game and surely have also defeated Ajax.

Sir Matt Busby's last match as the supremo of Manchester United would be on Saturday 17th May 1969, at Old Trafford against Leicester City. It would be his 1,141st match in charge of the club and, fittingly, he went out with a victory, 3-2 over a Leicester side who had suffered relegation under their manager, Frank O'Farrell. He would be very familiar with Manchester United in the early 1970s.

Pos	Club	Pld	W	D	L	GF	GA	Pts
10	West Bromwich Albion	42	16	11	15	64	67	43
11	Manchester United	42	15	12	15	57	53	42
12	Ipswich Town	42	15	11	16	59	60	41

As it was, the 1968/69 season ended in real disappointment and perhaps a foreboding of what the future held for a Manchester United side who would not be led by Sir Matt Busby for the first time in 24 years...

Chapter Twelve

CHANGING TIMES

Season 1969-70

The chapter heading is very pertinent to the world, and Manchester United in the summer of 1969.

The world was very different for a young Manchester United fan in 1969 to that of a young fan in 1960. The sixties remain the defining decade for Britain. The country had seen a transformation from a bleak, conservative place, only just beginning to forget the troubles of the Second World War, into a country seemingly full of freedom, hope and promise. The decade is often defined by its music. The decade had started with Emile Ford at number one with 'What Do You Want to Make Those Eyes At Me For?' and would end with Rolf Harris in the number one spot with 'Two Little Boys'. In between though, music had been transformed with the Beatles at the vanguard of the change. The early charts were dominated by rock and roll, and the early Beatles songs extended the genre. In 1967 though, the release of 'Sergeant Pepper's Lonely Hearts Club Band' marked a turning point, with innovative sounds and increasingly rebellious lyrics which every teenager could listen to on their transistor radio.

Nothing symbolised the technological change though as much as the moon landing. By the end of the decade, practically every house had a television, and since 1967 it was possible to watch in colour – marking a symbolic break with the black and white past. All around the world on July 20, 1969, the news that two Americans had walked on the Moon kept people glued to their television screens to witness this remarkable feat.

The 'space race' had been the focus of a peaceful propaganda war between the communist Soviet Union and the capitalist United States. The race captured people's minds to such an extent that the charts were topped by the Tornados in 1962 with Telstar which was number one in the UK and US (only the second British record to top the US charts) and of course by Frank Sinatra's immortal Fly Me To The Moon in 1964. The Soviet Union had taken the lead when Yuri Gagarin orbited the Moon on April 1961, the lead in the space race between Russia and America swayed back and forth throughout the 1960s but when Russian Alexei Leonov walked in space in 1965, the Soviets again demonstrated they were leading the way in space travel. Russia's success was too much for the pride of America, and in response, the Apollo Missions were developed. The programme did not start well, and America suffered a grievous blow in January 1967 when the first intended manned flight of the Apollo programme suffered a cabin fire in a test, killing the three crew. The Apollo programme though did recover,

124

and Apollo 9 and 10 made enormous strides, so much so that Apollo 11 was earmarked for the inaugural Moon landing. The three astronauts who flew the mission were, Neil Armstrong, Buzz Aldrin and Michael Collins, the first two would be the first men to set foot on the Moon while Collins flew the command module alone waiting for their return to Earth. While the landing was on 20 July the first walk on the Moon by Neil Armstrong was on 21 July with the three men, thankfully, returning to Earth on 24 July. Neil Armstrong's immortal words of *The Eagle has landed'* and *'One small step for Man, one giant step for mankind'* will live on forever. Frank Sinatra's 'Fly Me to the Moon' recorded in 1964 became immortalised through its close association with the Apollo missions. So strong did the association become that it was played on board Apollo 10, then becoming the first song heard on the Moon when played on a portable cassette player by Apollo 11 astronaut Buzz Aldrin after he stepped onto the Moon.

In the footballing world Manchester United, with their holy trinity of Best, Law and Charlton had provided the symbol of the changing decade. The club had entered the 60s with an uncertain future. Weak financially following the devastation of Munich and declining on the pitch. Despite that, the club's swashbuckling rise to the pinnacle of the world game had captured fan's hearts around the globe. The future looked bright for the club and its fans just as it did for all the optimistic children of the 60s. As we now know, despite all the progress of the 60s the UK would shortly be engulfed in strife and unrest – so too would Manchester United.

There are, of course, two Old Trafford's in M16, the one that is the home of the Lancashire County Cricket Club was there 53 years before Manchester United set foot on what became their 'Theatre of Dreams' Old Trafford. The cricket ground was firstly the home of the Manchester Cricket Club, becoming in 1864 the home of Lancashire County Cricket Club. At the end of the 1969 cricket season, Lancashire became the first winners of the new 40 over competition called the Sunday League. They had created a marvellously attractive side which included the future West Indies captain, Clive Lloyd and the flamboyant Indian wicket-keeper-batsman, Farouk Engineer. Led by as much a Lancastrian as you could get in Bolton man Jack Bond, this was to be the beginning a hugely successful period for Lancashire in one day cricket, a format which would change the whole game in the following years.

Meanwhile Manchester United prepared for their bright new future with a new man in charge of team matters following Sir Matt Busby's retirement, a Manchester United man through and through, Wilf McGuinness. Matt had not disappeared, however, as he now held the role of General Manager. Matt had been at pains to make clear that he would now have no role in team affairs but a symbol of his ongoing influence is provided by the fact that throughout Wilf's tenure Sir Matt Busby remained the voice of management in the club programme the 'United Review' with not one article being penned by Wilf. An interesting article in that most famous of club programmes detailed the amazing sales it achieved. It was a major part of the matchday experience, and the total sales of the previous 1968-69 season were recorded. The sales for that season's home matches totalled 1,554,504 copies sold in the ground. It covered 30 matches which included the closed-circuit TV match for the away leg of the European Cup Semi-Final against AC Milan. The actual second leg of that tie had seen 65,298 copies sold, while for the World Club Challenge against Estudiantes, 74,680 copies were sold, and this was a record for Manchester United programme sales. The average per game was an amazing 51,000.

On the field of play, Wilf must have hoped for a better start as, despite a point away at newly-promoted Crystal Palace, two very poor performances followed at Old Trafford resulting in heavy defeats against Everton and Southampton, 2-0 and 4-1 respectively. The performances certainly did not impress the huge Manchester United following. The match reports at the time were demining and reflected a worrying and increasingly vocal unease amongst United fans that had become accustomed to success. Reporting on the Southampton defeat in the Guardian, Arthur Hopcraft painted a poisonous atmosphere, noting that it was just four months ago that United had relinquished their European Cup title when knocked out of the competition at the semi-final stage: *This was a bitterly disillusioning defeat for Manchester United, only four months ago the holders of the European Cup. Sections of the home crowd slow-hand clapped in an indiscriminate derision. Law, barely able to make intentional contact with the ball, was booed repeatedly and with specific venom, the frequent opening of huge gaps between Southampton forwards and labouring Manchester defenders was observed with horrified silence, in which the disbelief hung as heavy as a visible cloud.'*

The dismal defeat in the game marked the last appearance for one of the club's unsung heroes from pre- and post-Munich, defender Bill Foulkes. Southampton had finished in seventh place the previous season and beat United at Old Trafford 2-1, completing the 'double' winning 2-0 at their home ground the Dell. They possessed one of the games finest traditional centre-forwards, Wales international Ron Davies, and he destroyed United, and centre-half Bill Foulkes in particular, scoring all four goals for Southampton. Let Roy Cavanagh give his tribute to a Manchester United great;

Bill Foulkes was part of the first Manchester United senior side I grew up with. He played number 2 - right-back, and as I stood on the ledge in the Stretford End paddock, he was always one of the closest to me. He was fondly called 'cowboy' by the men stood around me as he was quite bandy, never seeming to smile but hard as nails. He had made his debut just as the 1952 champions were going over the hill, but Bill was a firm part of the Busby Babes and their 1956 and 1957 championship-winning side. He was part of the side that played the last match of that team in Belgrade on the 5 February 1958, surviving the following day's air crash and was named as the captain of the new Manchester United as the club tried to regroup. By the time the first trophy after Munich was won, the 1963 FA Cup Final, Bill Foulkes was playing at centre-half, number 5.

Further championships were won in 1965 and 1967 giving Bill further shots at the European Cup. That he was there against Benfica in 1968 was a fitting tribute to a Manchester United great. In hindsight, he should have retired then as his few games in 1968-69 and the start of this 1969 season did him no justice. Bill Foulkes, is a true Manchester United Legend.'

A shadow team with no image

By ERIC TODD : Everton 3, Manchester United 0

With Sir Matt Busby seemingly looking over his shoulder and a mood of revolt amongst the fans, the pressure on Wilf McGuinness was immense. He didn't shy away from difficult decisions though and for the midweek return match away at Everton, Wilf McGuinness showed everybody he meant to be the boss, dropping Bobby Charlton, Denis Law, Shay Brennan and goalkeeper Jimmy Rimmer, and with Bill Foulkes also stepping down it was a much-changed side that took the pitch at Everton. It did not help that Everton were a fine side, indeed would be worthy champions that season, and they cruised into a 3-0 half time lead, which United did well to keep as the final score. The changes to the team were reflected in the headline in the following day's Guardian that branded the side as *a 'Shadow team with no image.'* This time the derision came from the opposition fans, *'How does one describe this latest execution? The prisoner could not even muster a hearty appetite, and Everton were in no mood for encouragement, sympathy or pity. Every mistake by United was greeted with derision: every time a United player, Best included, fumbled laughter rocked the terraces. And the chanted promises from their faithful followers that they'd support United evermore were delivered with defiance rather than the old conviction.'*

Let us hear what Wilf McGuinness thoughts were about those times in a typically humorous, though insightful, interview that he did with Roy Cavanagh in 1983: *'My big regret was that Sir Matt Busby didn't leave it another five years before retiring! The crown was there, and I was given it. I was overwhelmed when it happened; they never said do you want it, they just told me it was mine! A bit like Ronnie Corbett marrying Dolly Parton, the job was too big for me at 31! The papers made a big fuss of leaving Bobby and Denis out, although Bobby had been dropped by*

Sir Matt, along with myself in late 1959. Sadly for me, I broke my leg in the reserves and Bobby was back quick as a flash, and the rest is history.'

Wilf brought Bobby back quickly this time as well and recalled goalkeeper Alex Stepney. Having some money to move into the transfer market, with United desperately needing a replacement for Bill Foulkes, he bought the Arsenal and Scotland centre half Ian Ure for £80,000. Though the replacement was needed Wilf had much bigger plans if he had been given the backing. In that conversation with Roy Cavanagh, he disclosed that he wanted to also sign the England full-back Mick Mills from Ipswich Town, a future England international Colin Todd from Sunderland, and a young centre-forward from Luton Town called Malcolm MacDonald who would play in the reserves and develop!

The signing of Ian Ure, whilst not universally welcomed by Manchester United supporters, did put a stop to the poor performances and stopped the goals flying in, as 0-0 draws away at Wolverhampton Wanderers, and home to Newcastle United were finally rewarded by Wilf's first victory in his seventh match 3-1 at home to Sunderland at the end of August 1969.

Back in Manchester, Wilf McGuinness was to start a much-needed month of success. Away draws at champions Leeds United and at Arsenal, both 2-2, were included in an unbeaten run that also saw the then league leaders, Liverpool, beaten 1-0 at Old Trafford, Sheffield Wednesday beaten 3-1 at their Hillsborough home and as the month came towards its close, West Ham United, World Cup winners Bobby Moore, Geoff Hurst and Martin Peters and all, thrashed 5-2 at Old Trafford. Manchester United's World Cup winner, Bobby Charlton helped orchestrate this fine victory, which took United's unbeaten run to ten games in all competitions. The team had undergone a period of change with Bill Foulkes retired and Nobby Stiles, Pat Crerand, Denis Law all absent for various reasons, but with a very youthful team together with Charlton and a majestic George Best in tremendous form, they outplayed West Ham. All the goals were from former youth players, Burns, Kidd, Charlton and two from Best outweighing a brace from Hurst. The strains of 'Come on Georgie' ringing around Old Trafford from the 58,500 crowd to a Match of the Day audience must have been music to Wilf McGuinness's ears.

Included in the ten-match unbeaten run were two League Cup victories against Middlesbrough and Wrexham at Old Trafford. A single goal against Middlesbrough from yet another Old Trafford youth product, David Sadler saw United through in a competition they had not been competitive in during their two previous attempts. The next round brought Fourth Division Wrexham to Old Trafford, and they included David Gaskell in their goal. David had dropped out of league football after leaving Manchester United playing for non-league Bradford Park Avenue and Wigan before joining Wrexham. David Gaskell had been in the Manchester

United side that started the 1960s with an inglorious 7-3 defeat at Newcastle United, with Bill Foulkes having only just played his last match for the club, only Bobby Charlton and Shay Brennan were still playing for Manchester United as the decade was closing. David Gaskell had a fine match on his Old Trafford return before goals from Brian Kidd, and George Best took Manchester United further in the League Cup than they had ever been before.

Derby County had made a return to the First Division after a 16-year absence from top-flight football. Their return had been masterminded by the new management team on the block, Brian Clough and Peter Taylor. The 1969 side had made a great start to their return, led on the field by the superb Dave MacKay, the former Tottenham Hotspur and Scotland footballer. When United visited their Baseball Ground at the beginning of October 1969, the ten-match unbeaten run came to an end with a 2-0 defeat.

Progress in the League Cup against Burnley and Derby County, both after replays, took Manchester United into their first-ever Semi-Final in that competition, having suffered humiliating defeats at Bradford City by 2-1 and Blackpool 5-1 in their previous two attempts. The League Cup was often dubbed "Hardaker's Folly" from its beginning back in 1960 as the brain wave of League Secretary Alan Hardaker, a man who had crossed swords with Manchester United so fiercely in the mid-1950s when he totally opposed entry into the European Cup. When you look back, football owes Matt Busby a huge debt of gratitude for the way he fought to make sure Manchester United would not be refused entry when they had a chance to enter in the 1956 season.

As we near the end of the 1960s a man who played such a major role for Manchester United has hardly featured as he preferred to be outside the limelight. His name is Jimmy Murphy, the club's assistant manager through most of Matt Busby's tenure and alongside Wilf McGuinness during his time in charge of team affairs at Old Trafford. Jimmy Murphy's role at Manchester United must never be underestimated. But for him, Manchester United might have even folded, or at the very least gone down divisions after the Munich tragedy. Missing that fateful trip due to his duties as the Wales manager for a World Cup game against Israel, Jimmy was the rock on which Manchester United survived in the immediate days and months after the crash.

Matt Busby had seen Jimmy's passion when they met in the Second World War, and he became his right-hand man when he took over at Old Trafford after that war. Jimmy Murphy had been a very fine footballer for West Bromwich Albion and Wales in the 1930s, appearing in the 1935 FA Cup Final for West Bromwich Albion. His first role at Old Trafford was to run the Central League side, and after winning that title in the first season back after the war, Matt asked Jimmy who were the likely lads to be able to step forward to the first team. The answer was none!

Immediately the two men realised that they would have to cultivate their own talents for Manchester United and the famous youth policy for which the club is still known was developed. One stroke of luck was the creation of the FA Youth Cup from 1952 which proved a massive vehicle for Matt and Jimmy to see the progress their young hopefuls were making, and what progress! Winners of the first five competitions, the nucleus of what became known as the Busby Babes was formed.

Throughout Matt Busby's success and heartaches, Jimmy Murphy was a constant thread. His love of the club and the respect and love that some of the greatest footballers ever to grace Old Trafford had for him are a testament to what a man he was. Wilf McGuinness certainly knew that, as he, along with all the stars of the 50s and 60s, credited Jimmy Murphy with not just helping, but completely forming their careers. There are not enough words to express what Manchester United owe to this man from South Wales who never sought personal limelight, got on with his job and developed so many footballers.

The progress United had made in the 1969 Football League Cup, produced an all Manchester League Cup Semi-Final against City, with the first leg at Maine Road. Before that though, the sides met in a league match at the same venue, with a very disappointing ending for United! A 4-0 defeat was the worst Wilf McGuinness had suffered in his new role, but at least he had the opportunity of putting that right very quickly with the prospect of leading United to a Wembley final in the League Cup.

Manchester battle really boiling . .

UNITED STORM AT DISPUTED LEE PENALTY

United had been without the injured Nobby Stiles all season and his return just before the first-leg was welcome news for Wilf. Showing his tactical nous, Wilf put Nobby into the number ten shirt and altered United's formation from a 4-2-4 to a more defensive 4-3-3. Even so, Manchester City went into an early lead with a Colin Bell goal, but this time Manchester United were far more equipped to handle the City side. Nobby Stiles, in particular, was in no mood to take any nonsense from the City forwards and let them know he was most certainly back! The second-half saw United take control of the match and a Bobby Charlton equaliser was the least they deserved. With the clock ticking to the 90th minute a coming together between Francis Lee and Ian Ure produced a notorious flying fall by the City player, only for referee Jack Taylor to point to the penalty spot. Lee got up to score the winner on the night. George Best left the referee in no doubt of his feelings as they went down the tunnel at the end, which resulted in a lengthy ban for United's Irish star, though he would be able to play in the second leg. Best wasn't alone in questioning the penalty, as after the game even City's assistant manager Malcolm Allison agreed, commenting *'I thought it was harsh.'*

As a 'warm-up' to the second leg, United travelled to Anfield to play Liverpool in a league fixture and produced a most memorable performance with Wilf McGuinness's tactics again to the fore as he masterminded a fine 4-1 victory against a Liverpool side in third place in the league. Wilf recalled Pat Crerand after a spell in the reserves, and the Scot responded with fine probing balls which the eager forward line of Morgan, Charlton and Best lapped up. The performance was the perfect preparation to give United the confidence to overturn their one-goal deficit against City in the League Cup semi-final tie.

A return to Wembley would have been the perfect ending for the 1960s for Manchester United, but sadly, in front of a 63,418 strong Old Trafford crowd on Wednesday 17 December 1969, there was to be no happy ending. City had gone one-nil up on the night to give them a 3-1 aggregate lead before United fought back marvellously. The least experienced United player, 21-year-old Paul Edwards, playing only his fifth match scored an unlikely equaliser from his right-back position and by the second-half United were in full flow. A Best shot was parried by City goalkeeper Joe Corrigan only for Denis Law to sweep home and put United 2-1 up on the night and level at 3-3 in the tie. As extra-time loomed an error by goalkeeper Alex Stepney settled the tie in City's favour. A direct free-kick to City taken by Francis Lee was saved by Alex only for the ball to unaccountably come loose allowing Mike Summerbee to put City level at 2-2 gifting City a 4-3 victory in the overall tie.

The mention of Paul Edwards at right-back for Manchester United confirmed the ending of Shay Brennan's career at Old Trafford. Shay's was a most interesting time at Manchester United. He had not looked like breaking through by 1958, but then the Munich tragedy saw him play as outside-left in the emotional FA Cup tie with Sheffield Wednesday, the first match after the crash. Not only did he play, but Shay scored twice in United's 3-0 victory. Over the years, Shay became a very useful utility player before settling as the permanent right-back as the league titles of 1965 and 1967 were won. He was in that position on the memorable European Cup victory over Benfica in 1968, by which time Shay Brennan had become the first player to be selected for the Republic of Ireland despite not having been born in that country. Having been born in Manchester, he had qualified via his parents' heritage. Shay, Bobby Charlton and Wilf McGuinness had formed close personal friendships as they came through Manchester United's system but by the end of the 1960s, his time at Old Trafford and as a footballer was fast coming to a close. Shay Brennan though, was one of only two players to have played in Manchester United's first match and last match of the 1960s, Bobby Charlton being the other. Shay played in the last match of 1969 at Sunderland, with his last ever Manchester United appearance following in the 3rd round FA Cup tie at Ipswich Town on the first Saturday of 1970.

A final act of the 1960s in a political sense occurred the day before the second leg League Cup Semi-Final on the 18th December 1969 when the House of Lord's voted to abolish the death penalty in England, Wales and Scotland; Northern Ireland would do so in 1973.

The final acts in a football sense would see Manchester United play Wolverhampton Wanderers in a Boxing Day Old Trafford match, and travelling to the North East to play Sunderland on the 27th December 1969. Both matches finished in draws, 0-0 and 1-1 respectively, ironic though that the last football match of the iconic 1960s Manchester United would play would be in the same region as their first match of that decade over at Newcastle United, happily the 1-1 draw ended the decade on a better ending then the 7-3 defeat started it!

For the visit to Roker Park, Sunderland, 36,504 spectators witnessed the last football of the 1960s seeing this Manchester United side gain a 1-1 draw thanks to a Brian Kidd goal; Stepney, Edwards, Brennan, Crerand, Ure, Sadler, Morgan, Kidd, Charlton, Burns and Best. As the 1970s arrived, Manchester United were in 11th position in the First Division having played 26 league matches and accumulated 28 points from nine victories, ten draws and seven defeats, scoring 38 goals and conceding 37 goals.

Pos	Club	Pld	W	D	L	GF	GA	Pts
10	Arsenal	27	7	14	6	31	28	28
11	Manchester United	26	9	10	7	38	37	28
12	Newcastle United	26	11	5	10	35	36	43

The team would enter a new decade under the leadership of Wilf McGuinness but still very much under the influence of Sir Matt Busby.

Chapter Thirteen

RED RECOLLECTIONS

Personal Memories of United in the Sixties from two long-standing
Manchester United supporters

Mike Carney

If you were aged 16 or 17 in 1960, as I was, you were truly blessed. The whole of your youth ahead of you, to be spent in the swinging sixties. The generations before us had spent their time fighting wars and looking for work. I left St Ambrose College in 1960, and not a minute too soon! Never particularly enjoyed my days there and was looking forward to a job with the Northwich Guardian as a junior reporter. However, in those days, you did what your parents thought was a "respectable" job and on my mother's instruction, I ended up working at an accountants in Knutsford, which if it did nothing else, it introduced me to "the big, bad, world."

My obsession as a child had been Manchester United, and Rock n Roll music (in that order). United in 1960 were an average side, having been decimated by the Munich Aircrash, two years earlier, but making small steps in the right direction. Ironically at the end of the 1960s, they were also an average side but making bigger steps in the wrong direction! The first game I recall from the 60s was an FA Cup game at Anfield when Liverpool were still in the old second division. I stood on the Kop in front of the children's pen, and even in those days got a "missile" in the back from one of the little darlings when United scored in a fairly easy 3-1 win. However, we were beaten in the next round at OT by Sheffield Wednesday who became regular cup opponents in the following couple of years.

Musically, in my opinion, the death of my great hero, Buddy Holly, really was *"The day the music died"* in 1959. There had been two or three years of bland music with boring ballads from the likes of Mark Wynter and Craig Douglas. However, one night in June 1962, I went to the Saturday night dance, at the Memorial Hall in Northwich, where I watched a group who at the time played a lot of Rock n Roll music as well as some of their own stuff which blew me away. Little did I know that I was witnessing, at least to the wider public, the birth of the Beatles!

Later that year, in October, a reminder, if one was needed, that the world could indeed be a dark place occurred when nuclear weapons were discovered in Cuba, just ninety miles from the USA. The next couple of weeks, the world stood on the edge of nuclear destruction until the Russians effectively backed down and agreed to remove the missiles. How serious it was sunk in when my father, normally very much the optimist, declared *"It's looking black"*.

Meanwhile, my trips to OT were restricted to night matches as I played football in the early 60s on a Saturday afternoon. However, between Boxing Day 1962 and the late Spring of 1963, all football was postponed as the icy grip of the "Big Freeze" took its toll. I was able to see all United's FA Cup games up to the 6th round as they were played in the week at OT. Having closely avoided relegation in 1963, United's improvement this season was complemented during the bad weather by the signing of Pat Crerand from Celtic who many considered the "final piece of the jigsaw" Indeed, in my opinion, United gave their best Wembley performance, in my time, by beating Leicester City 3-1 to win the FA Cup for the first time in fifteen years. I was fortunate to see the game by obtaining a ticket from Hartford FC who I was playing for at the time.

The dances at the Memorial Hall were attracting youths from all over Cheshire in the early sixties, as the likes of the Beatles, Rolling Stones, Hollies and many more regularly appeared in the small market town. However, that still left time for my trips to the Sale Locarno, the Ritz with its bouncy dance floor, Belle Vue and a few more Manchester nights out.

Holidays in the early sixties for young people were still confined to Britain and the most popular places for youths in the North West were Blackpool, Butlins and the Isle of Man. In July 1963 I had a memorable week at Butlins in North Wales where I met a lad called Terry Brennan from Manchester who turned out to be the brother of Shay Brennan, the United full-back.

By November 63, I had moved to work for Marley Tile in Delamere and owing to a busy workload, decided to work late one Friday evening. I arrived home about 7.30pm to be told by my father that President John F Kennedy had been assassinated in Dallas. The sadness that enveloped the country spread to OT where United lost to Liverpool the following day.

The most memorable United games in 1964 were a trilogy of FA Cup ties against Sunderland. The first one saw United scoring twice in the last five minutes to earn a 3-3 draw. The replay at Roker Park saw another thrilling encounter with United equalising at the end of normal time and extra time to secure a 2-2 draw. Having missed the trip to Sunderland, I drove over the moors for the second replay at Huddersfield which was yet another thrilling game. Trailing at half time to a goal from Dominic Sharkey, the Reds clicked into gear after the interval to run out comfortable 5-1 winners! However, the exertions from these three games caught up a few days later when West Ham knocked us out in the semi-final 3-1 on a quagmire of a pitch at Hillsborough.

In the Autumn of 1964, I eventually moved to ICI, which whilst was still office work, which I never particularly enjoyed, at least paid decent money. I was to remain there for the next 30 years. As I referred to earlier, not the most interesting of occupations but one which allowed me to retire at 50 with a "golden handshake" and a pension.

In the newspapers in the mid-sixties, there were occasional references to a civil war in Vietnam which was to grow into a major conflict for the USA. I remember being concerned that the UK could be dragged into it and that yours truly would be belatedly doing some kind of National Service! Ultimately it was a war which the USA couldn't win and didn't.

On the football front, in 1965, United claimed their first league title since Munich beating Leeds on goal difference. The vital game was at a windswept Elland Rd towards the end of the season when John Connelly scored the only goal of the game. This meant United returning to the European Cup for the first time in seven years. They would ultimately, disappointingly be eliminated in the semi-final by a virtually unknown team from Yugoslavia, called Partizan Belgrade. Everyone expected United to win the European Cup as they had, in the previous round, thrashed Benfica 8-3 on aggregate! At this time Benfica were arguably the best team in Europe. This, in my opinion, was the season the great side of Best, Law and Charlton was at its peak.

Having seen an advert by Mancunia Travel for a trip to Lisbon to watch the Benfica game, I thought that £29 for hotel, flight, and match ticket was pretty reasonable. Probably the equivalent of a week's wages at the time but nevertheless, I had to go!

Having never flown before, I concentrated on the flight. The plane was an Argonaut, and the pilot was Captain Marlow. Nothing memorable about that other than a year later, the same plane, piloted by the same Captain crashed in the middle of Stockport. Most of the passengers died, but the Captain survived. However, back to Benfica 66. On the way to the Estadio de Luz, we passed loads of excited Benfica fans, who to a man held up a hand, indicating a five-goal win for their favourites. Of course it didn't turn out like that, and a George Best inspired United produced what in my humble opinion was a performance that was the closest United have ever got to perfection, ironically winning 5-1!

Having missed the coach back into Lisbon, my uncle and I met a Benfica fan in a bar who kindly drove us back to our hotel. He said that United were the best team he had ever seen on the strength of that performance. An amusing antidote to the trip was an old boy from Salford walking up and down the aisle of the plane on our return, with his cap outstretched, *"collecting for the driver."*

In the Summer, I saw most of the group World Cup games at OT and Goodison. The games at OT turned out to be pretty ordinary, but the games involving Brazil, Hungary, and Portugal at Goodison were memorable. It has always been a feeling of regret that I turned down the opportunity of a ticket for the final offered to me by a workmate at ICI.

The following season, 1966/67, saw United regain their title from Liverpool and I was fortunate to be at Upton Park where the Reds sealed it with a 6-1 over the Hammers. This, of course, meant another crack at the Holy Grail, the European Cup. This United team could be a bit inconsistent, but most of the time, with Best, Law and Charlton at their peak, they were arguably the most thrilling team we've ever had.

It was my belief that it was around this time, that music changed, but not for the better when the likes of the Beatles departed from their Rock n Roll roots. Whilst I liked the Sergeant Pepper album, for me it was the watershed, and popular music was never to be the same again. Music was reflected by Society and many of the problems we see in the 21st century had their beginnings in the mid-sixties. Authority, in particular, being challenged by the younger generation.

In the Summer of 1967, we had the Arab/Israeli war which I have to admit concerned me, particularly when a work colleague suggested that my "holiday" might be spent in the Middle East. However, it was a short conflict, and normal service was resumed. Also, Enoch Powell gave his "Rivers of Blood " speech. In the autumn of 67, I rashly got engaged to Jennifer and started to save for our " bottom draw" We celebrated by purchasing a ring in Manchester and going on to OT to watch United beat Coventry 4-0. It was a taste of things to come.

United coasted through to the quarter-finals of the European Cup, with a little scare against Sarajevo, winning 2-1 in the second leg at OT, after a goalless draw in Yugoslavia. The quarter-final in the Spring of 1968, was against Gornik from Poland, and a two-goal lead saw them through after a 1-0 loss in Katowice on a snowbound pitch.

Martin Luther King Jr was assassinated, and Alexander Dubcek made an unsuccessful attempt to break Czechoslovakia free from the iron grip of the Soviet Union. Medically, the first heart transplant was performed by Christian Barnard in South Africa.

The semi-final draw pitted United against Real Madrid and the opportunity to avenge the 1957 semi-final defeat to the Spaniards. The first leg at OT saw a Best goal give the Reds a slim one-goal lead to take to the Spanish capital. I recall thinking how much I'd love to be there, but I didn't have the money. Of course, I did have the *"bottom drawer"* money and after giving it a bit of thought, decided to use it to get to Madrid. This was the beginning of the end for my engagement to Jennifer, although it did drag on until the end of the year.

The trip to Madrid turned out to run Lisbon 66 a close second. I stayed at the Cuzco Hotel, over the road from the Bernabeu in a suite with lounge etc for two nights. Match ticket and flight for £30! Spent the first afternoon strolling around the Bernabeu, taking a video with a cine camera which I'd bought with the excess from my *"bottom drawer"* money! This video earned me a considerable amount of money thirty-odd years later when ITV did programmes such as *"Reds in Europe"*. The following morning, myself and one or two pals turned up outside the Fenix Hotel where the team were staying, and I was pleased to get some quality film of them getting on the bus for training.

When the game started, the atmosphere was electric with 125,000 baying for United's blood, and by half-time, they had almost got it with a 3-1 lead. In all honesty, it could have been 6-1, so poor were the Reds. Fifteen minutes or so into the second-half Real started to strut, probably thinking the job was done, and with it the atmosphere disappeared, United upped their game and scored a couple of goals from Sadler and of all people Bill Foulkes. Try as they may, Real couldn't get back into the game, and despite the nerve-jangling last fifteen minutes, they never looked like scoring again!

After the game, we headed to the Fenix Hotel, and despite not seeing the players, we joined in the celebrations with the English Press. I recall speaking to Danny Blanchflower, who probably hit the nail on the head when he commented on how lucky United had been. The image will always remain with me of Louis Edwards hugging a *"Stretford Ender"* who looked like he was wearing the same clothes he had had on for weeks!

The final at Wembley was just two weeks later, and surprisingly, I found tickets for myself and one or two family members easy to come by. The big day arrived, and I travelled down to meet my cousin Terry who lived in Kent. It was the same day as the Derby and I recall backing the winner, Sir Ivor ridden by Lester Piggot. It was a very warm evening, and standing with the United fans behind the goal at the Tunnel End was draining. The game was pretty ordinary until extra time when United quite easily overpowered a Benfica side who had probably run out of steam, to win 4-1. The Holy Grail had been achieved, and I'm sure everyone over twenty had a tear in their eye as they remembered the events of ten years earlier. I believe that it was achieved at the eleventh hour as this team had started a decline which ended in the club's relegation in 1974.

Before the celebrating had died down, at the beginning of June, over in Los Angeles, the Kennedy family suffered yet another tragedy as Robert Kennedy, who was a Presidential candidate, was gunned down in a hotel by Sirhan Sirhan. This was not the end of family tragedy for the Kennedys as accidents continued to haunt them through to the 21st century.

On a personal note, in January 1969, I dated a girl that I'd met a few months earlier, of all places, in church. She was different than anyone else I had met during the previous ten years or so and the relationship took off to the extent that we were married in August 1969, only seven months after our first date. Our song was *"Fly Me to the Moon"* as Neil Armstrong had become the first man to set foot on the moon in July 1969. Aeronautically, Concorde first took to the skies, and within a couple of years, it was possible to fly to New York in 3 hours. Fifty years later, it takes 6 hours, and they say we have progressed.

The 68-69 season had commenced with a trip to Dublin to watch United comfortably beat Waterford in the European Cup. My next trip was to watch a boring 0-0 draw with Rapid Vienna in the Austrian capital in March of 1969. However, Vienna was one of the most beautiful cities I have visited. The match was at the Prater Stadium which evoked memories of the film The Third Man and Harry Lime etc. Again, the day before the game, we walked into the ground and had a kick about on the pitch for a few minutes before we were ejected. Don't think that would happen today!

The Reds relinquished their hold on the European Cup at the hands of AC Milan at OT when modern technology may have given them a reprieve when a *"goal"* from Denis Law was adjudged not to have crossed the line!

Music, in my opinion, had changed with the Summer of Love and Flower Power. Rock n Roll as I knew it had all but disappeared. With the exception of Queen, I have not been stirred to this day by any bands since the mid-sixties! I still follow tribute bands who play 50s and 60s music, usually at the Memorial Hall in Northwich. So, the sixties came to a conclusion and left us with the most wonderful of memories! Which years were the most memorable? Sport had to be United's European Cup win in 1968. Music had to be 1962 when I first watched the Beatles in my hometown of Northwich. World event had to the terrifying two weeks in October 1962, when the world teetered on the edge of destruction during the Cuban missile crisis and finally, personally meeting and marrying Patricia in 1969.

Pete Molyneux

Oh, what a night,
Late December back in '63,
What a very special time for me

Memory is an essential part of what makes us human; that hard-drive in our head that recovers images and thoughts of people, places, events at will or randomly. Yet it is still one of the most complex of human attributes with neurologists only now beginning to understand how our brain processes memories. Looking at it crudely it seems to me that the power of memory is enormous for most of our lives but struggles to focus in our early years and fades again if we survive into old age.

Memories from the first seven years of my life are just a collection of disparate events and happening, most of which were driven by what my parents arranged for me. That's commonplace for all of us. There is very little perspective around the timing of those events or any depth to their purpose. But all that changed when I was eight, the 25 May 1963 to be precise. From that date on, I started to have some say in determining the things in life that inspired or excited me. The day was a fairly ordinary Saturday for young Pete living in Whitefield a smart Manchester suburb. That afternoon I went to play football in the street outside our house with my slightly younger neighbour David Hibbert. It was all very amateur stuff, one v one, a few attempted dribbles and shots at goals which were, in fact, the gateposts of our various neighbours. I liked football and had just started playing it at primary school, but I wasn't very good and knew little about professional football teams.

My dad was watching a match on TV, so we popped in to ask him who was playing. He told me it was the FA Cup Final at Wembley Stadium and Manchester United were up against Leicester City. I knew that my dad liked United, so when Dave and I went back outside and decided to pick which of the teams we wanted to be, I picked Man United. Luckily, Dave was happy to be Leicester. For the rest of that afternoon, and for the rest of my life, Manchester United were MY team. United won the FA Cup that day, and I'd been bitten by the bug from the moment my Dad said the name.

I started buying Charlie Buchan's Football Monthly, and when the new season began in August '63, I followed United's fortunes through radio, TV and my dad's reports when he returned from home matches. I asked my Dad if I could go with him to Old Trafford for a game. He deferred the decision to my mum; understandably she was concerned that terraces packed full with 55,000 partisan supporters were one step too far for son and heir. As a compromise my dad took me to reserve team matches at Old Trafford in the Central League. For a while that scratched the itch but the real excitement in that 63/64 season came with United's run in the FA Youth Cup. These were night matches, and I learned how floodlit games brought an extra dimension to the excitement, especially in cup competitions. Christmas came a week early for me that year. On Wednesday 18 December 1963 my dad took me to see the FA Youth Cup 2nd Round tie between United and Barrow under the Old Trafford lights.

The club used to only open the old 'Main Stand' now the Bobby Charlton Stand, but even the opening rounds of the Youth Cup matches would attract 3-4,000 spectators. Our memories are powered by our senses primarily, and that first cup game left three indelible recollections. One was the smell of liniment; a balm nicknamed 'footballers rub' which players of that era massaged onto their legs to relieve pain, stiffness, aches and strains in their muscles. The Main Stand housed the players' changing rooms, and as you approached the turnstiles, the smell of liniment wafted from a couple of small windows and filled the air. The fans needed their winter-warmer just like the players so once inside the ground my dad would buy us both cup of Bovril - a thick, salty, beef drink. Basically, it smelt of cows but if you could get past that it didn't half keep you warm. The third attack on my senses was the vision of the Old Trafford pitch. From high in the stand it looked such a dark, vivid green and took a young lad's breath away. When United's team ran out in their blood-red shirts the contrast against the green was magical. But the real magic was provided by 17-18 year olds that the club had creamed from the best school teams across the UK.

Matt Busby's philosophy after becoming manager in 1945 was to build teams mainly hewn out of home-grown talent. His 'Babes' had won the inaugural FA Youth Cup in May 1953 then dominated the competition for the next four seasons. Those players provided the backbone of the sides who became English League Champions in '56 and '57. The tragedy of the plane crash at Munich halted that pipeline of top-class talent. But by 1963 the manager and club were back on their feet, driven on by the memory of the players who had perished. The FA Cup win at Wembley against Leicester proved a vital landmark that Manchester United would soon be a force again. None of us knew in autumn of 1963 that the Class of '64 would provide the bedrock for Busby's glittering side of the Swinging Sixties which would also win two English titles before rising to the greatest challenge in club football and lift the European Cup.

The Youth team that played Barrow in December '63 contained future stars Jimmy Rimmer, Bobby Noble, John Fitzpatrick and Willie Anderson with David Sadler and Johnny Aston waiting in the wings. But the star who shone the brightest that evening was George Best. The slightly built Irishman simply lit up the Old Trafford night with dazzling dribbling skills, ball control that bordered on witch-craft and balance that beggared belief. He would continue to light up my life for the next decade and way beyond his playing days. George Best was, is and always will be my hero. Any player one who's ever worn the shirt for Manchester United has been my hero and some like Law, Charlton, Cantona, Keane, Robson, Giggs, Rooney and Ronaldo have sparkled brighter in the Old Trafford galaxy than others. But George Best arrived on the football scene at the same time I began a life-long love affair with the game. The heady cocktail of Best's magic and football-dependence forge a bond no other player could surpass.

George had signed amateur terms with United in May '61. In the opening United Review of 61-62 several new juniors were mentioned by name but the only a vague reference applied to Bestie "a number of boys from 'across the water' are showing their paces in trials, and any that measure up to the high United standard will be retained, and no doubt be catching the eye in these notes as the season progresses" No doubt George measured up, and soon his name started to appear in reports of the 'B' team then after Christmas '61 in the 'A' team. The first half of 62-63 saw our young prodigy back in the 'B' side, but again after the turn of the year, he was playing and scoring for the 'A's. On 24 April 1963 he made his debut for the Youth Cup team in a 3-2 win over Newcastle. Summer 1963 saw United sign George Best on professional terms, but the club were keeping their rising star under wraps. Matt Busby handed George a debut against West Brom on 14 September 1963, but despite an impressive game the skinny Belfast lad was back in the reserve and youth sides.

By the time the Barrow cup game arrived, George was forcing Busby's hand with displays beyond his years. United won the match 14-1 (no that's not a misprint, United scored FOURTEEN times). All five forwards contributed to that total. Bestie grabbed a hat-trick but had to settle for third place in the scoring stakes; Ken Morton went 'nap' with 5, Frank McEwen hit four whilst Anderson, and Albert Kinsey notched one each. McEwen and Morton would be the first to acknowledge Best's skills in creating the opportunities for their nine strikes. The match doesn't figure large in United's history, but young Pete had had a taste of honey that he couldn't live without for the rest of his life. On the way home I couldn't stop talking about the match and my new hero Georgie Best. My dad was excited too but struggled to get a word in.

My burgeoning love of football had been accompanied by a growing interest in pop music culture, in particular, the Beatles and the Stones. Those early grainy black and white TV images of Jagger and Richards, Lennon and McCartney coupled with foot-stomping songs resonated in a way my toy soldiers and train sets never did. A week before that trip to Old Trafford, I went into Woolworths in Cheetham Hill Manchester and bought my first ever record. Pocket money had come on stream from my parents and the Beatles' I Want To Hold Your Hand seemed the ideal way to part with it. The final month of 1963 had triggered two of the three passions that would consume my formative years. I was only 9, man would walk on the moon before the opposite sex entered my universe, but for now music and football rocked my world. I had Best and The Beatles – my life had meaning.

United's first XI were hammered 0-4 and 1-6 at Everton and Burnley over Christmas '63. In the return game against The Clarets two days later Matt Busby played youngsters Anderson and Best on either wing. United won 5-1; George played in 26 of the remaining 28 league and cup fixtures that season. United were fighting for the league, FA Cup and European Cup Winners' Cup, so George didn't play in the next three rounds of the Youth Cup. United were drawn at home in every round, and each matchday couldn't come quick enough. Blackpool led twice but were beaten 3-2, Sheffield United cast aside 2-0 and a plucky Wolves team eliminated 3-2. That took United into the semi-finals and a local 'derby' against City over two legs. By the time the home leg took place on 8 April, the first team were out of all three major competitions, so Jimmy Murphy played Best. Albert Kinsey scored a hat-trick in the 4-1 victory watched by a crowd of around 30,000.

The semi-finals gave me my first taste of a Manchester 'derby'. Even at that level, there was an extra edge to the game, a different buzz in the ground and more heated discussions with City fans in the playground the next day. When my Dad got us tickets for the 2nd leg at Maine Road I really thought I'd arrived. Here I was going to watch a United 'away' match even though it was only the Youth Cup and just nine miles from my house. The tie attracted a great crowd of circa 21,000 and both sides serving up a cracking game and a feast of goals. United won 4-3 to go through to the final 8-4 on aggregate. Best and Sadler, who by now were both first team regulars, each scoring twice. United's first FA Youth Cup Final since May 1957 would feature Swindon Town who had their own version of George Best in Don Rogers, a speedy left-winger with a mop of black hair who could score goals too. The away leg was too far for me and my dad to travel on a Monday night, and there was no coverage on TV or the radio. So we had to wait for the newspapers the following morning to find out the score. I was up a 6.30am and down to the newsagents in record time to pick up a paper, then ran back home and tell my dad United had drawn 1-1. Rogers had given The Robins the lead on 31 minutes, but Bestie equalised 20 minutes from time. The matched was watched by 17,000 fans.

So, it was all set up for the second leg at Old Trafford on Thursday 30 April 1964, manager Murphy sent out the following team: Rimmer; Duff, Noble (C); McBride, Farrar, Fitzpatrick; Anderson, Best, Sadler, Kinsey, Aston. After joining the Football League from the Southern League in 1920 unfashionable Swindon spent 43 years in the lowest division. But something was stirring in sleepy Wiltshire. A young manager called Bert Head, who would go on and lead Crystal Palace into the top-flight at the end of the 60s, was bringing some focus to Swindon Town. His regime produced stars such as John Trollope, Mike Summerbee, Bobby Woodruff, Ernie Hunt, Keith Morgan, Rod Thomas, David 'Bronco' Layne. The Youth Cup Final was a more tense affair than the 25,563 Old Trafford faithful had expected. But two goals from Sadler, each a minute either side of half-time broke the underdogs' hearts. Bruce Walker halved the deficit on 68 minutes, but 120 seconds later Sadler secured his hat-trick before Aston notched a fourth towards the final whistle.

The atmosphere was superb; you could feel it meant so much to the players and the fans. The trophy was presented to United not far from our seats, and the crowd invaded the pitch to get a closer view. This was the most exciting moment I'd had in my life up to that point and a memory to savour forever. History shows that clubs winning the Youth Cup may see a couple of players progress through to regular first-team football. That Youth team produced seven which was exceptional and stirred memories of Busby's first bunch of babes a decade earlier. After 1964 it would be another 28 years before United lifted the Youth Cup again, this time with the fabled class of 1992. Manchester United still hold the record for most FA Youth Cup wins in the history of the competition with ten successes. Our club is still synonymous with producing great young talent.

So, my introduction to football at Old Trafford was good, but it wasn't quite the real thing. I'd avidly follow the results of the first team and dream of seeing them play live. I kept pestering my dad, but he was having none of it. In May 1964, I got close to a first-team fixture. Bert Trautmann, City's legendary German keeper, was given a testimonial and invited United as the opponents. My dad and uncles were split 50:50 between United and City and were all going to the match. There was talk of a spare ticket, and for a few days I prayed I could join them, but one of my dad's friends had it, and I was left at home. So near yet so far; it was torture.

I lived close to Sedgley Park Rugby Club in Whitefield. I wasn't interested in rugby, but I used to set out the flags around the pitches before the games which earned me half a crown (12.5p) each weekend. For a ten-year-old, it was a good little earner. Before leaving the house to do that job, if United were playing at home I'd ask if I could go to the match with my dad. I'd become used to apologetic rejections and often didn't wait for the reply before heading towards the door. But on Saturday, 26 September 1964, I heard my dad say, "what do you think, mum?" I couldn't believe it was even up for debate.

Moreover, I couldn't take in her reply when she said, "go on then" smiling and winking at my dad, "but don't let him out of your sight whatever you do!" I raced round to the rugby club to tell them I couldn't put the flags out today......I was going to Old Trafford to see Manchester

United play Tottenham Hotspur!

We parked up somewhere on Trafford Road and set-off walking to the ground. Every fourth or fifth step, I'd have to run to keep up with my dad. I was so full of anticipation and excitement that I started to wonder if I'd built it up too much in my mind. Could the experience end up as one of life's great disappointments? I needn't have worried. As we made our way up the steps and onto the uncovered Popular Side on United Road, the teams were just coming out of the tunnel. My dad lifted me onto his shoulders and there before my eyes were my heroes – Pat Dunne, Shay Brennan, Tony Dunne, Paddy Crerand, Bill Foulkes, Nobby Stiles, Georgie Best, David Herd, John Connolly, Denis Law and Bobby Charlton. Not in black and white on a small TV or a photo in a magazine. They were LIVE in glorious red and white. There were 53,000 at the match, and the atmosphere was like nothing I'd experienced or could have imagined. My dad wormed his way through the packed terraces and got us close to one of the crash barriers. He sat me on the iron bar and stood behind, making sure I didn't fall.

I already knew that matches between United and Spurs in the 60s were something special. Both had become glamour sides, but that glamour had a steely backbone. United had ruled the roost in the mid-50s, but the crash at Munich allowed Wolves to win titles in '58 and '59. But they were blown away by a Spurs side that became the first team in the 20th century to win the coveted English League and Cup double in 1961. Managers Busby and Bill Nicholson believed their teams were there to win games but also entertain the public and this fixture had a magic all of its own. After finishing runners-up in 1964, United started the new campaign in poor form with just one win in the first six matches. But as newcomers Pat Dunne (goalkeeper) and John Connolly (right-winger) settled in so started a run of 19 unbeaten league and cup games. Tottenham at home was the sixth match in that run and United purred that day with a line-up of:

P Dunne; Brennan, A Dunne; Crerand, Foulkes, Stiles; Connelly, Charlton, Herd, Law, Best.

The crowd roared every United move, and it seemed to lift the Red-shirted heroes to another level. There must have been some Spurs fans in the ground, but I don't remember seeing or hearing any in this partisan mass. When the goals went in the noise nearly blew me away. Everyone around just went ballistic. I found it an intoxicating potion of excitement and fear. I clung to my dad, cheering like mad, but holding on really tight, so we didn't get separated. Paddy Crerand was the unlikely hero that day scoring twice with long-range shots. He only scored ten league goals in over 300 matches, so I was privileged to witness one-fifth of them in my first game. A wet and dull day had given way to bright sunshine as the second half began. United's passing was crisp and accurate with an urgency to get forward as quickly as possible at every opportunity, which was great to watch. Tottenham's defending was suspect at times, and Denis Law's presence anywhere in their half made them very nervous. In the 59th and 89th minutes, they twice conspired to let in Law as they passed across the back four. In between Spurs scored a consolation, but United ran out 4-1 winners.

Dad and I survived each of the United goals huddled around that crash barrier. At last, I'd seen United play! I couldn't contain my excitement, when I got home I followed my mum all around the house trying to tell her about it, but all she was really interested in was that I'd come back in one piece. After that I went with my dad to virtually all United's home games, missing only five over the next three seasons. In that time United would win two league titles to re-establish themselves amongst England's top teams. The football was magical, not in every game, but there was rarely a dull moment. Entwined in those thrilling domestic league and cup games were matches against foreign sides in the Inter-Cities Fairs Cup and the European Cup. Those fixtures took excitement to another level against teams with exotic-sounding names and kits with different colours and styles to those we were used to in Britain. When I used to walk home from school daydreaming, I'd imaged I was playing for United in those European ties, helping them fight back from one or two-goal deficits in the football cathedrals of Europe.

I'd also dream that my team would conquer Europe as they had done English football. That dream was fulfilled in May '68 with a trip to Wembley with my Dad for the 4-1 win over Benfica. These dreams fuelled a devotion to United that became an absorbing passion and at times, an obsession. That dedication became the backdrop to my life, and just like life, it brought with it some incredible highs and a few tragic lows. It still does, seven decades later.

*Authors' note: Roy & Carl recommend all readers to buy a copy of Pete's great book —
'Ta Ra Fergie'. A brilliant read!*

Chapter 14

CLOSING THOUGHTS

To complete the season Manchester United had started in 1969, they would finally finish in eighth position, an improvement of three places for Wilf McGuinness in his first full season in charge of team matters on Sir Matt Busby's last season. They had also finished a couple of places higher then rivals Manchester City, while Wilf had guided the side to a second semi-final appearance, this time in the FA Cup. There, Leeds United ended Wembley dreams for United but only after a titanic struggle, and a fixture pile-up that takes some believing.

The semi-final was played on Saturday 14 March 1970 at Hillsborough, home of Sheffield Wednesday and, like the previous time these two clubs had met five years earlier at this stage, ended in a grinding 0-0 draw. The replay was arranged for a week the following Monday 23rd March at Villa Park, home of Aston Villa. This was then the first of five matches Manchester United played in eight days, two of which were semi-finals of the FA Cup, and one was a local 'derby' against Manchester City! The game at Villa Park also finished 0-0, this one after a further gruelling 30 minutes extra time. The second replay was then arranged for the Thursday night over at Burnden Park, home of Bolton Wanderers played on Maundy Thursday the 26th March. A goal finally came in the early stages, but sadly for Manchester, scored by Billy Bremner the Leeds United captain. There then followed the Easter surge of fixtures, with United losing 2-1 at home to Manchester City, then playing Coventry City at Old Trafford and finishing with a trip to the City Ground to play Nottingham Forest on Easter Tuesday. A draw with Coventry and a welcome 2-1 win at Forest ended those five matches in eight days.

During the 60s decade, Manchester United finally fought back from the devastation of the 1958 Munich disaster, going on to achieve their greatest ever success by winning the European Cup ten years on from that disaster. They competed in a World Club Championship match, won two Football League Championships, won the FA Cup, had two further semi-final appearances in the European Cup, and once in the Inter-Cities Fairs Cup, were runners up in the Football League twice, losing semi-finalists four times in the FA Cup, and once in the Football League Cup, along with jointly sharing two Charity Shields and winning the FA Youth Cup.

For the most part, of course, they were led by Sir Matt Busby, although the super-human efforts of his assistant Jimmy Murphy can never be overlooked. One of those two's protégés, Wilf McGuinness succeeded Sir Matt for the last season in the 60s decade. Player wise, Manchester United had at times on the field of play three European Footballers of the Year,

Bobby Charlton, Denis Law and George Best, the only football club to ever have that many at the same time. Bobby and George would also be awarded the Footballer of the Year trophy in England in the 1960s.

In a continuation of their famed youth policy which stretched throughout the 60s decade, footballers such as Nobby Stiles, George Best, Bobby Noble, David Sadler, John Aston, Brian Kidd and Jimmy Rimmer were produced, with any signings being pieces for the jigsaw of success. Interestingly, their signings would have made the positions one to eleven as follows; Alex Stepney, Tony Dunne, Noel Cantwell, Pat Crerand, Ian Ure, Maurice Setters, Willie Morgan, Graham Moore, David Herd, Denis Law and John Connelly, only Ure, Morgan and Moore not winning winner medals in the 60s decade at Manchester United.

While the 1960s certainly changed many people's lives, the question remains was it a real-world or fantasy after so much despair, decay and anger of the post-war years? The 60s saw man orbit, then walk on the Moon, would see a transformational attitude to popular music from the young, see that same generation explore fashion and colours to a new degree, had travel options no other generation could have dreamed of, but also see horrific violence towards people via wars and assassination's. The unbridled optimism of the 60s soon turned sour and quickly evaporated in the early 1970s when the harsh reality of industrial disputes, economic decline, social unrest and over in Northern Ireland, sectarian violence, made people wonder if the 'Swinging Sixties' had ever really existed.

The parallels with Manchester United are clear. It is worth reflecting on the state of the club as they entered and left the decade. On 1 January 1960 United stood in 10th place in the Football League with a squad still decimated by the Munich disaster and without the financial muscle to quickly fill the gaps. Ten years later, on 31 December 1969 United stood in 11th place in the Football League. Despite the club's perilous situation at the start of the decade, Sir Matt Busby had led the team to undreamt of success playing a thrilling style of football that endeared the club to fans around the world. In principle, the club left the decade in an immeasurably stronger period than they entered it. Few would have predicted anything but further success for the club despite a drop in performance following the lifting of the European cup in 1968. As we now know it did not turn out that way, decline had set firmly in and, remarkably, the most famous club in the world suffered a humiliating relegation just four years later in 1974. The road back was hard and long, and the next league title would not be until 1992-93 under United's second legendary manager – Sir Alex Ferguson. There are no doubt parallels with today's United in the post-Ferguson years and lessons need to be learnt if the road ahead now isn't going to be equally tough.

The focus of this book though is the sixties and regardless of what came before it and what would come to pass there was no better decade to be alive, no better time to enjoy football, and no better club to support than Manchester United.

They say if you remember the 1960s you were not really there, well this has been an account of what it was like...

STATISTICS

Club and Individual Honours

	Competition		Year			
1	European Cup	Winner	1967-68			
1	European Cup	Semi-Finalist	1968-69			
1	FA Cup	Winner	1962-63			
4	FA Cup	Semi-Finalist	1961-62;	1963-64;	1964-65;	1965-66
2	League Division One	Champion	1964-65;	1966-67		
2	League Division One	Runner-up	1963-64	1967-68		
2	FA Charity Shield (Jt winners)	Winner	1965;	1967		
1	Central League	Winner	1959-60			
1	FA Youth Cup	Winner	1963-64			

European Player of the Year	
Denis Law	1964
Bobby Charlton	1966
George Best	1968
FWA Footballer of the Year	
Bobby Charlton	1965-1966
George Best	1967-1968

Overall Record by Competition

Competition	Played	W	L	D	For	Against
League Division One	422	193	126	103	867	549
FA Cup	50	29	9	12	83	75
European Cup	25	17	4	4	52	26
League Cup	12	5	3	4	21	7
Fairs Cup	11	6	2	3	20	19
UEFA European Cup Winners Cup	6	3	2	1	22	4
FA Charity Shield	3	0	1	2	9	5
Intercontinental Cup	2	0	1	1	2	1
Total	**531**	**253**	**148**	**130**	**1076**	**686**

Appearances

Alphabetical list of every appearance, by every player, from 1st January 1960 to 31 December 1969.

Name		League			FA Cup			League Cup			Inter-Cities Fairs Cup		Cup Winners Cup		European Cup			Other		Total		
		Apps	Sub	Goals	Apps	Sub	Goals	Apps	Sub	Goals	Apps	Goals	Apps	Goals	Apps	Sub	Goals	Apps	Goals	Apps	Sub	Goals
Anderson	Willie	7	2	0	0	0	0	1	0	0	0	0	0	0	0	0	0	2	0	10	2	0
Aston, Jr.	John	112	8	23	4	0	0	9	0	0	0	0	0	0	8	0	1	0	0	133	8	24
Best	George	241	0	94	29	0	9	9	0	2	11	2	2	2	21	0	6	4	1	317	0	116
Bradley	Warren	20	0	3	3	0	1	0	0	0	0	0	0	0	0	0	0	0	0	23	0	4
Bratt	Harold	0	0	0	0	0	0	1	0	0	0	0	0	0	0	0	0	0	0	1	0	0
Brennan	Shay	274	0	3	33	0	0	4	0	0	11	0	2	0	11	0	0	3	0	338	0	3
Briggs	Ronnie	9	0	0	2	0	0	0	0	0	0	0	0	0	0	0	0	0	0	11	0	0
Burns	Francis	75	2	5	3	0	0	6	0	0	0	0	0	0	10	1	1	1	0	95	3	6
Cantwell	Noel	123	0	6	14	0	2	0	0	0	0	0	4	0	3	0	0	2	0	146	0	8
Carolan	Joe	19	0	0	3	0	0	1	0	0	0	0	0	0	0	0	0	0	0	23	0	0
Charlton	Bobby	382	0	119	49	0	10	8	0	1	11	8	4	4	25	0	6	7	0	486	0	148
Chisnall	Phil	35	0	8	8	0	1	1	0	0	0	0	1	0	0	0	0	2	1	47	0	10
Connelly	John	79	1	22	13	0	2	1	0	0	11	5	0	0	8	0	6	0	0	112	1	35
Cope	Ronnie	24	0	0	3	0	0	1	0	0	0	0	0	0	0	0	0	0	0	28	0	0
Crerand	Pat	266	0	9	32	0	4	3	0	1	11	0	6	0	24	0	0	5	0	347	0	14
Dawson	Alex	46	0	30	4	0	3	3	0	1	0	0	0	0	0	0	0	0	0	53	0	34
Dunne	Pat	45	0	0	7	0	0	1	0	0	11	0	0	0	2	0	0	1	0	67	0	0
Dunne	Tony	311	0	2	41	0	0	10	0	0	11	0	6	0	23	0	0	5	0	407	0	2
Edwards	Paul	5	1	0	0	0	0	2	0	0	0	0	0	0	0	0	0	0	0	7	1	0
Fitzpatrick	John	66	6	3	8	0	1	5	0	0	0	0	0	0	7	0	0	0	0	86	6	4
Foulkes	Bill	325	3	6	41	0	0	3	0	0	11	0	6	0	19	0	2	4	0	409	3	8
Gaskell	David	87	0	0	16	0	0	1	0	0	0	0	0	0	1	0	0	5	0	110	0	0
Giles	Johnny	97	0	10	13	0	2	2	0	0	0	0	0	0	0	0	0	1	1	113	0	13
Givens	Don	5	2	1	0	0	0	1	0	0	0	0	0	0	0	0	0	0	0	6	2	1
Goodwin	Freddie	1	0	0	1	0	1	0	0	0	0	0	0	0	0	0	0	0	0	2	0	1
Gowling	Alan	10	2	1	0	0	0	0	1	0	0	0	0	0	0	0	0	0	0	10	3	1
Gregg	Harry	132	0	0	15	0	0	2	0	0	0	0	2	0	5	0	0	0	0	156	0	0
Haydock	Frank	6	0	0	0	0	0	0	0	0	0	0	0	0	0	0	0	0	0	6	0	0
Herd	David	201	1	114	35	0	15	1	0	1	11	6	6	3	8	0	5	2	0	264	1	144

Appearances (cont)

Alphabetical list of every appearance, by every player, from 1st January 1960-31 December 1969.

Name	League			FA Cup			League Cup			Inter-Cities Fairs Cup		Cup Winners Cup		European Cup			Other		Total		
	Apps	Sub	Goals	Apps	Sub	Goals	Apps	Sub	Goals	Apps	Goals	Apps	Goals	Apps	Sub	Goals	Apps	Goals	Apps	Sub	Goals
Heron, Tommy	2	0	0	0	0	0	0	0	0	0	0	0	0	0	0	0	0	0	2	0	0
James, Steve	22	0	1	6	0	0	1	0	0	0	0	0	0	2	0	0	0	0	31	0	1
Kidd, Brian	90	1	24	7	0	2	6	0	2	0	0	0	0	16	3	3	2	0	121	4	31
Kinsey, Albert	0	0	0	1	0	1	0	0	0	0	0	0	0	0	0	0	0	0	1	0	1
Kopel, Frank	8	2	0	0	0	0	0	0	0	0	0	0	0	2	0	0	0	0	10	2	0
Law, Denis	233	0	141	34	0	34	3	0	1	10	8	5	5	18	1	14	5	1	308	1	204
Lawton, Nobby	36	0	6	7	0	0	1	0	0	0	0	0	0	0	0	0	0	0	44	0	6
McMillan, Sammy	15	0	6	0	0	0	0	0	0	0	0	0	0	0	0	0	0	0	15	0	6
Moir, Ian	45	0	5	0	0	0	0	0	0	0	0	0	0	0	0	0	0	0	45	0	5
Moore, Graham	18	0	4	1	0	1	0	0	0	0	0	0	0	0	0	0	0	0	19	0	5
Morgan, Willie	50	0	10	5	0	1	5	0	0	0	0	0	0	4	1	1	2	0	66	1	12
Morgans, Kenny	2	0	0	0	0	0	0	0	0	0	0	0	0	0	0	0	0	0	2	0	0
Nicholson, Jimmy	58	5	5	5	0	1	3	0	0	0	0	2	0	0	0	0	0	0	68	6	6
Noble, Bobby	31	0	0	2	0	0	0	0	0	0	0	0	0	0	0	0	0	0	33	0	0
Pearson, Mark	50	0	10	3	0	1	0	0	0	0	0	3	1	0	0	0	0	0	56	0	12
Pinner, Mike	4	0	0	0	0	0	0	0	0	0	0	0	0	0	0	0	0	0	4	0	0
Quixall, Albert	112	0	38	13	0	4	1	0	0	1	0	3	2	0	0	0	0	0	130	0	44
Rimmer, Jimmy	8	0	0	0	0	0	0	0	0	0	0	0	0	2	1	0	1	0	11	1	0
Ryan, Jimmy	21	2	4	1	0	0	0	0	0	0	0	0	0	2	0	0	0	0	24	2	4
Sadler, David	164	5	20	6	1	4	9	0	0	0	0	0	0	14	0	0	2	0	195	6	24
Sartori, Carlo	15	4	1	3	0	0	1	1	0	0	0	0	0	1	0	0	0	0	20	5	1
Scanlon, Albert	17	0	3	3	0	1	3	0	0	0	0	0	0	0	0	0	0	0	23	0	4
Setters, Maurice	159	0	12	25	0	0	2	0	0	1	0	6	2	0	0	0	1	0	194	0	14
Stepney, Alex	139	0	0	9	0	0	8	0	0	0	0	0	0	15	0	0	3	0	174	0	0
Stiles, Nobby	288	0	17	35	0	0	8	0	0	5	0	5	0	23	0	2	3	0	367	0	19
Tranter, Wilf	1	0	0	0	0	0	0	0	0	0	0	0	0	0	0	0	0	0	1	0	0
Ure, Ian	23	0	1	0	0	0	7	0	0	0	0	0	0	0	0	0	0	0	30	0	1
Viollet, Dennis	49	0	29	4	0	0	2	0	1	0	0	0	0	0	0	0	0	0	55	0	30
Walker, Dennis	1	0	0	0	0	0	0	0	0	0	0	0	0	0	0	0	0	0	1	0	0

Top 20 Appearances

	Name		Apps	Sub	Goals
1	Charlton	Bobby	486	0	148
2	Foulkes	Bill	409	3	8
3	Dunne	Tony	407	0	2
4	Stiles	Nobby	367	0	19
5	Crerand	Pat	347	0	14
6	Brennan	Shay	338	0	3
7	Best	George	317	0	116
8	Law	Denis	308	0	204
9	Herd	David	264	1	144
10	Sadler	David	195	6	24
11	Setters	Maurice	194	0	14
12	Stepney	Alex	174	0	0
13	Gregg	Harry	156	0	0
14	Cantwell	Noel	146	0	8
15	Aston, Jr.	John	133	8	24
16	Quixall	Albert	130	0	44
17	Kidd	Brian	121	1	31
18	Giles	Johnny	113	0	13
19	Connelly	John	112	1	35
20	Gaskell	David	110	0	0

Three players played in every season in the sixties: Bobby Charlton, Bill Foulkes and Shay Brennan. Bill Foulkes would not appear in the seventies, and Shay Brennan would play just one game. Bobby Charlton would go on to play for United until 1973 – a remarkable player and an unrivalled servant to the club. One player stands out from the list as a comparatively unsung hero. Tony Dunne, with 442 appearances, *'Mr etc.'* as he modestly called himself – a manager's dream. Most that saw him play rate Tony Dunne as one of United's greatest full-backs.

Top 20 Goalscorers

	Name		Apps	Sub	Goals	Goals per Game
1	Law	Denis	308	0	204	0.66
2	Charlton	Bobby	486	0	148	0.30
3	Herd	David	264	1	144	0.55
4	Best	George	317	0	116	0.37
5	Quixall	Albert	130	0	44	0.34
6	Connelly	John	112	1	35	0.31
7	Dawson	Alex	53	0	34	0.64
8	Kidd	Brian	121	1	31	0.26
9	Viollet	Dennis	55	0	30	0.55
10	Sadler	David	195	6	24	0.12
11	Aston,Jr.	John	133	8	24	0.18
12	Stiles	Nobby	367	0	19	0.05
13	Crerand	Pat	347	0	14	0.04
14	Setters	Maurice	194	0	14	0.07
15	Giles	Johnny	113	0	13	0.12
16	Morgan	Willie	66	0	12	0.18
17	Pearson	Mark	56	0	12	0.21
18	Chisnall	Phil	47	0	10	0.21
19	Foulkes	Bill	409	3	8	0.02
20	Cantwell	Noel	146	0	8	0.05

When it comes to goalscorers, there is no doubt that Denis Law is king. With 204 goals in the decade, he is clear of his nearest challenger Bobby Charlton. With a remarkable record of 0.66 goals per game he was United's most important signing of the decade. The early sixties was a period in which United were blessed with quality strikers. David Herd and Dennis Viollet have the same strike rate of 0.55 goals per game and were ably supported by Alex Dawson whose record of 0.64 per game is only just below that of the king. The lower end of the table is noteworthy also. Only nine players managed to score over 30 in the decade. Noel Cantwell and Bill Foulkes make the list, with a total of just 8 and strike rates of a goal every 18 and 50 games respectively!

Home Attendances

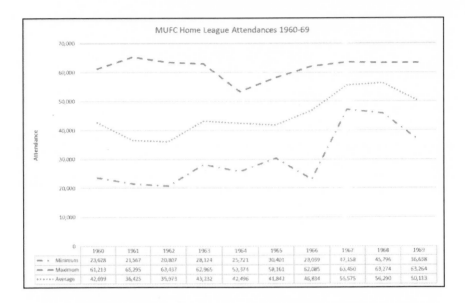

MUFC Home League Attendances 1960-69									
	1960	1961	1962	1963	1964	1965	1966	1967	1968	1969
Minimum	23,628	21,567	20,807	28,124	25,721	30,401	23,039	47,158	45,796	36,638
Maximum	61,213	65,295	63,437	62,965	53,374	58,161	62,085	63,450	63,274	63,264
Average	42,699	36,425	35,973	43,232	42,496	41,842	46,834	56,575	56,290	50,113

The lowest average home crowd for United was 35,973 in the 1962-63 season with the highest average being 56,290 in the 68-69 season. A feature of the early part of the decade was the variation in attendances with a crowd of just 20,807 in 1962 against a highest that year of 63,437. It was an era with very few season tickets, and spectators could pick and choose their matches on the day – a sharp contrast with today's crowds – overwhelmingly season ticket holders and zero availability on the day.

Another contrast is the comparison between FA Cup and League Crowds. Throughout the decade the FA Cup was the highlight for spectators. United's crowds for the FA Cup were as follows......

FA Cup Record					
P	W	L	D	F	A
50	31	11	8	101	57

FA Cup Winners 1963, Semi-Finalists 1962, 1964, 1965, 1966

FA Cup Crowds (Home)				
Lowest	40,000	09-Jan-65	Round 3	Chester City
Highest	66,350	20-Feb-60	Round 5	Sheffield Wednesday
Average	56,810			